VGM Opportunities Series

OPPORTUNITIES IN
ACCOUNTING CAREERS

Martin H. Rosenberg

 **VGM Career Horizons**
a division of *NTC Publishing Group*
Lincolnwood, Illinois USA

Library of Congress Cataloging-in-Publication Data

Rosenberg, Martin H., 1942–
    Opportunities in accounting careers / Martin H. Rosenberg.

        p.   cm. — (VGM opportunities series)
    Includes bibliographical references.
    ISBN 0-8442-8577-3 (hardbound): $12.95. — ISBN 0-8442-8578-1
(softbound): $9.95
    1. Accounting—Vocational guidance. I. Title. II Series.
    HF5657.R652   1990
657'.023'73—dc20   90-38431
                                                                   CIP

657
R

c. 1

Published by VGM Career Horizons, a division of NTC Publishing Group.
©1991 by NTC Publishing Group, 4255 West Touhy Avenue,
Lincolnwood (Chicago), Illinois 60646-1975 U.S.A.
All rights reserved. No part of this book may be reproduced, stored
in a retrieval system, or transmitted in any form or by any means,
electronic, mechanical, photocopying, recording or otherwise, without
the prior permission of NTC Publishing Group.
Manufactured in the United States of America.

0 1 2 3 4 5 6 7 8 9 VP 9 8 7 6 5 4 3 2 1

ABOUT THE AUTHOR

Martin Rosenberg began his professional career as a senior lecturer in anthropology at the American Museum of Natural History in New York City. After three years of teaching at the museum and City College of New York and New York University, he joined the staff of the Education and Examinations Division of the American Institute of Certified Public Accountants. In his nearly nine years with the AICPA, Rosenberg managed the functions of state CPA society relations and, in his last institute assignment, was manager of the Professional Ethics Division.

In 1977, Rosenberg became executive director of the Illinois CPA Society, the state professional organization with headquarters in Chicago and an office in the state capital, Springfield. Its membership numbers more than twenty-three thousand. In his capacity as executive director, he administers a staff of sixty.

He is a member of the Joint Conference Committee of the American Institute of CPAs, National Association of State Boards of Accountancy and State CPA Societies, which is currently studying the regulation of the CPA profession. He also serves on the AICPA state society Government Affairs Committee and the AICPA Advisory Committee of Quality Review for CPA Firms.

Rosenberg is a member of the Board of Directors of the American Society of Association Executives Foundation, and in the Chicago Society of Association Executives, he is chairman of the Government Affairs Committee. He received CSAE's highest honor, the 1989 Samuel B. Shapiro Award for Outstanding Service and Accomplishments in Association Management.

ACKNOWLEDGMENT

The author wishes to acknowledge the assistance of Jane Kelledy, who researched and updated the lists and sources contained in this book.

CONTENTS

CHAPTER 1

THE ACCOUNTING PROFESSION

The 1990s will see the impact of a global economy, connected by a sophisticated network of electronic computer communications. Information will be available to organizations of all sizes. Securities and financial markets will operate on a twenty-four-hour basis. News and its impact will be transmitted simultaneously throughout the world. There will be broad economic opportunities for businesses to expand and serve the European Common Market as well as Eastern Europe. The turbulence of the 1980s is being replaced by the decade of opportunity. Information will be the most valuable commodity. Access to relevant data and news will be critical to the success of a business.

Coming with these changes is the growing concern over how to regulate an international marketplace. What is a reasonable balance between governmental oversight and the various professions' and trade groups' own forms of self-regulation? Will corporate codes of ethics become commonplace and more stringently enforced? How will the free trade agreements between nations serve to change the states' rights system in the United States, with its myriad of different laws and statutes regulating CPAs and other licensed professionals?

The accountant's green eyeshade stereotype image will be only history as the 1990s unfold. True, there will always be a level of record keeping that is routine and purely mathematical in function, but these tasks will be performed using networked microcomputers and clerical personnel, not trained accountants. Data entry will require large numbers of employees whose tool is the computer, not the typewriter or individual calculator. Accountants of the 1990s will have undertaken to obtain more education than their predecessors. Included in this education are subjects such as computers, international business law, and ethics, with an increased emphasis on communication skills, both verbal and written. Professional accountants will be distinguished by their academic credentials and sought-after achievements such as passing the uniform CPA examination.

Accounting professionals will be at the forefront of designing information systems, giving a company's management the data it needs to report on its operations and make decisions. With larger computer systems linking many parts of a business, the need for strengthened internal controls, including computer security, presents challenges for accounting professionals. Accountants of the 1990s will prepare for a career in which they function as critical coordinators of information systems and overseers of management controls, and when they serve as independent auditors, attesting to the reasonableness of a company's financial statements. Whether working inside a company or in a CPA firm, accountants will share many common concerns, especially the peculiar needs of specific industries and types of businesses. Accounting educators have the unique responsibility of preparing students to meet these new challenges. Governmental accountants will be assuming more responsibilities for monitoring how taxpayer dollars are spent. Perhaps even the accounting profession's recommendations for simplification of United States tax laws and regulations will lead to needed change.

Accounting is financial mapmaking. It organizes, charts, and presents complex transactions and financial interrelationships in a reliable fashion. Not all information is necessarily useful. Of equal or greater importance is the accountant's assurance that information is verifiable, objective, accurate, and compiled in an unbiased way. In this complex economic world, information is critical, and the ''information czars'' are the professional accountants.

With the advent of computerized record keeping, the tasks required of bookkeepers, who work under the supervision of accountants, shifted from the tedious routine of making entries manually to the fast, efficient, but equally repetitive computer input duties now required. The knowledge of accounting at the data-entry level can be minimal, and little judgement is needed to record raw source data. Elementary bookkeeping can be simply learned with one or two years of high school training. In fact, on-the-job training can produce sufficient bookkeeping knowledge to perform at this level.

This book is intended for the student who aspires to participate in the unparalleled opportunities for accountants in the 1990s. Training in accounting and other business fields, such as computer science at the college level, is required for those who hope to tap these opportunities.

The recognized mark of competence in professional accounting is obtained by passing the CPA examination. Large numbers of CPAs are employed in industry, education, and government positions, not solely in public accounting practice. The CPA certificate awarded by the fifty-four licensing jurisdictions in the United States has become an important benchmark of educational achievement for top management financial positions and an absolute requirement for the practice of public accounting.

The financial world and government bodies at the federal, state, and local levels place great importance on the work of independent public accountants. Financial statements audited by CPAs are mandated by public and private agencies in the interest of investors, credit grantors, and taxpayers. For example, the New York Stock Exchange requires that corporations having their capital stocks or bonds listed for trading on the exchange furnish their stockholders with financial statements audited by independent public accountants at least annually. The Securities and Exchange Commission (SEC) of the federal government also requires that companies coming under its jurisdiction furnish financial statements bearing the opinion of independent public accountants for review and approval before new securities of those companies can be offered to the public. In addition, the commission requires all companies coming under its jurisdiction to file with the SEC annual reports bearing the opinion of independent public accountants. Growing reliance on public accountants is very evident at all levels of government, particularly where an independent examination of organizations expending taxpayer revenues is involved. Many such audits are required under the federal or state laws providing for these social programs. Many accountants find rewarding careers in government accounting positions, and their skills in organizing and analyzing financial information are important to the efficient operation of these public agencies.

HISTORY OF ACCOUNTING

Accounting in Ancient Times

A number of modern accounting concepts, such as internal control procedures as well as management accounting techniques, can be traced to prebiblical times. Archaeologists and cultural anthropologists have found evidence in some form as far back as 3600 B.C. in ancient Babylonia. There have even been discoveries of small handmade polished objects dating back thousands of years earlier, objects that are surmised to have been used as gaming devices or scoring pieces. The first indication of modern bookkeeping dates from about 600 B.C. with the business and household practices of ancient Rome.

The Bible, which is considered to cover events between 1800 B.C. and A.D. 95, contains references to accounting. The concept of accounting controls, for example, appears to have been used to help ensure that an enterprise not be defrauded either by its employees or by outsiders. In references to the building of a temple, it can be inferred that accounts would have been kept if the contractors were less than honest. Also, accounting was viewed as a means of checking performance, as in a parable in which an owner, hearing that his steward is wasting money, says, "What is this I heard from you? Draw me up an account of your stewardship." In the area of resolving disputes between parties, the Bible states, "These are things you should not be ashamed of—keeping strict accounts with a traveling companion." The idea that keeping accounts would serve to reduce unnecessary conflict between parties seems evident. In sum, it appears that the Bible points out that financial accounting is necessary to avoid fraud, to monitor agents or employees, and to reduce conflicts over resources. The Bible also has references to budgeting and the budgeting process and many managerial-related topics. For example, one reference asks, ''Which of you here intending to build a tower would not first sit down and work out the cost to see if you had enough to complete it?''

The Development of Modern Accounting

In the fifteenth century, Italy was known for its commerce and trade, and, in 1494, Luca Paciolo, a Franciscan monk, published a treatise on double-entry bookkeeping, ''Tractatus XI, Particularis de Computis,'' included in his *Summa de Arithmetica*. Although this treatise is the first-known significant writing on the subject, it is interesting to note that Paciolo did not claim that he invented or discovered bookkeeping but wrote about it as the method in use in Venice at that time. His statement gives us every reason to believe that double-entry bookkeeping had been the technique of financial recording by merchants and businessmen in Italy for some time prior to 1494.

Almost one hundred years later is the earliest recognition of financial record keeping as a specialized occupation. The records show that in Venice, in 1581, the first college of accountants was organized with power to regulate entry into the field. Admission requirements then bear a striking resemblance to regulations for entering the profession today. An applicant was required to submit a certificate of fitness signed by a magistrate, serve a six-year apprenticeship with a practicing accountant, and pass an examination.

Italy apparently was the leader in accounting for many years, but it appears that about the eighteenth century, Scotland and England took the lead. Public accounting in a limited way was recognized in those countries during the latter part of the eighteenth century, but by the middle of the nineteenth century, there is tangible evidence of a separate profession of accounting developing. In 1854, a society of Scottish accountants, the Society of Accountants in Edinburgh, was formed, and not long thereafter, its members were designated as chartered accountants. In 1855, a similar society was organized in Glasgow, and during the next twenty-five years, several other accounting organizations came into being in various cities in England and Scotland. However, the Institute of Chartered Accountants of England and Wales, which was formed in 1880, probably had more to do with shaping the future of the accounting profession than did any of the other organizations up to that time.

During the 1800s, many British entrepeneurs made substantial financial investments in American enterprise and sent their public accountants to the United States to obtain objective reports. One English accountant was dispatched to the American Midwest during this period to look after the interest of the British owners of the Chicago, Burlington, and Quincy Railroad. He spent the rest of his working life in that railroad's accounting department. In this fashion, many other British accountants migrated to the New World, helping to establish the profession on this side of the Atlantic.

By the 1880s, there were a number of individuals and small firms practicing public accounting in this country, and in 1887, the first organization of public accountants, the American Association of Public Accounts, was formed. This association, with many changes over the years, is now the American Institute of Certififed Public Accountants (AICPA), the largest and probably the most influential organization of professional accountants in the world.

Twentieth Century Accounting

The passage of the income tax law of 1913 and establishment of the Securities and Exchange Commission in 1933 were tremendously stimulating to the accounting field in the twentieth century. Further, as government tapped corporations and individuals for income and other taxes and the tax code became ever more complex, experts were needed to delve into corporate and individual finances to determine what taxes were owed as well as for the purpose of helping to plan activities to minimize tax obligations. Similarly, the auditing duties of accountants were expanded and enhanced as the Securities and Exchange Commission, the stock exchanges, and the accounting profession began to give more and more attention to the types and amounts of information corporate financial statements were required to impart. Research and study of accounting and auditing principles governing such matters were pressed forward with increasing intensity.

The need to interpret and explain the complexity of modern financial matters was not confined to large corporations alone. Nonprofit organizations, small companies, and individuals, too, were affected. In matters relating to taxes, investments, and estate planning, many people found it difficult to cope on their own and increasingly turned for help to accountants, especially to individual practitioners and those in smaller accounting firms. Today, for many families, the accountant has become an indispensable financial adviser.

FIELDS OF ACCOUNTING

Where do you find accounting jobs? Accountants use their skills in working for a wide variety of business, financial, governmental, and educational entities. Within these organizations, accountants generally specialize in what they do. The major fields are public accounting, management or industry accounting, government accounting, and accounting education. As employees in major fields, accountants progress through phases of increasing specialization, such as cost accounting, auditing, taxation, management consulting services (particularly in the area of computer systems), and personal financial planning.

Public Accounting

When engaged in public accounting, accountants render professional services to the public as sole practitioners or as members of public accounting firms. Public accounting is considered a profession similar to the profession of medicine or law in its basic requirements for entry into practice.

Public accounting has as its foundation the rendering of audit services. The importance of independent audits to investors, financial institutions, regulatory agencies, and taxpayers has resulted in public accountants being licensed in every jurisdiction in the United States. In auditing, CPAs examine clients' financial statements and express a professional opinion on them. The role of independent attestor is unique to CPAs. It is also necessary for CPAs to develop expertise in matters of taxation, computers, federal and state laws, and management operations. Noncertified accountants may generally perform accounting, tax, and management services to clients, but in virtually all states they are restricted from performing the audit function unless licensed as public accountants. Public accounting firms have been the most active recruiters of accounting graduates at colleges and universities. On campus, public accounting is considered to be one of the best ways to develop broad exposure to a wide variety of businesses and to have a chance to acquire specialized skills at an early stage in a career.

A beginning public accountant can expect to progress through several staff-level positions. Starting as a staff accountant includes helping those in charge of an audit engagement conduct the examination. The typical next level would be as an in-charge accountant with responsibility for planning and conducting an audit engagement. A major step forward comes in promotion to manager. This position carries responsibility for the supervision of the in-charge accounting staff. The last promotion is to partner of the firm. As partner, there is increased responsibility for supervision of managers and a direct participation in the decisions and operations impacting the firm itself. While certainly not only limited to public accounting, communication skills and self-confidence are important to real success in this field. Later in this book we will explore, in greater depth, the skills required for a successful public accountant.

Management/Industry Accounting

Management accountants are sometimes referred to as industry or private accountants as contrasted with their colleagues in public accounting. Titles such as controller, financial vice-president, treasurer, director of internal audit, chief accountant, cost accountant, internal auditor, accounting supervisor, and director of taxation describe the widely known and highly visible positions in the operations of a company. By the very nature of employment with a particular industry, management accountants automatically become specialists very quickly. It may be in accounting for a utility company, banking or other financial institution, retailing, manufacturing, or specialty service industry such as insurance. While basic training as an accountant is required for entry into management accounting, specialized knowledge has to be acquired for the particular industry in which the accountant is employed. This training is obtained through continuing education courses and on-the-job experience. The CPA credential, as well as the MBA and specialized degrees in taxation, are valuable tools in seeking a career as a management accountant. The management accountant is responsible for developing, producing, and analyzing data useful for making business decisions and for reporting to internal and external interested parties. A solid educational background in accounting and related disciplines is essential for the person who wants to move to a top management position in industry.

Government Accounting

Government accountants are hired to work in an extremely wide range of positions in federal, state, and local governments. The federal government employs CPAs and non-CPAs in many of its agencies, such as the Internal Revenue Service, the General Accounting Office, and the Defense Contract Audit Agency. Similar to public accounting and management accounting, these positions invariably involve general accounting skills and specialization in more narrowly defined areas. The Internal Revenue Service, among other responsibilities, audits individual and corporate tax returns. The General Accounting Office is the key audit agency of the United State Congress. It assists in investigations to determine compliance with government policy and regulations covering government programs and the expenditure of public funds. Audits of defense contractors can involve many millions of dollars and are the major responsibility of the Defense Contract Audit Agency.

Accounting Education

Accounting educators are in great demand today. Supplying the increased need for trained accountants in public accounting and industry has put a significant strain on the availability of educators in accounting departments. Accounting educators are on the faculty of community colleges, colleges of business administration, and graduate schools of business. A growing trend is toward the establishment of schools of professional accountancy similar to those of other professions, such as architecture, law, and medicine. After beginning their careers as instructors, accounting educators may eventually be promoted to professorships.

We have only begun to gain some insight into the career opportunities available to accountants. The remaining chapters of this book will help you understand each of the fields of accounting, determine the skills and resources you will need, and get a picture of the structure of the accounting profession and the professional organizations to which accountants belong.

CHAPTER 2

PERSONAL SKILLS AND PROFESSIONAL ATTRIBUTES

A professional is more than just a skilled worker. In addition to possessing knowledge, the professional must exercise sound judgement, be committed, and show evidence of a practiced expertise. Interpersonal skills are an important factor in the success or failure of a professional. The ability to effectively communicate, orally and in writing; to have poise and self-confidence; and to exhibit an aggressive but not overbearing style are important qualities that instill confidence in employers or other users of a professional's services.

To best evaluate your abilities, begin by identifying and defining the various skills to be assessed. These will normally include personal, management, and technical skills. A professional can also be characterized as possessing, at a minimum, the following attributes: sound judgement, consistent ethical behavior, strong interpersonal skills, a level of knowledge in prescribed specialized areas, dedication and loyalty to the profession and to colleagues in other professions, and a responsibility to serve the public.

PERSONAL EVALUATION

Personal qualifications consist of aptitudes, interests, and characteristics. These are not easy to appraise or to describe in definite terms; however, they should be evaluated, and there are certain techniques that can be applied to give a good idea of the probability of an individual's success in an accounting career.

Although self-appraisal is difficult, this is the first step that should be taken. Comparing your aptitudes, interests, and characteristics with those of practicing accountants as outlined in this chapter will assist you in arriving at a sound decision regarding a career in accounting.

Self-appraisal can be accomplished in several ways. High schools and colleges generally offer students counseling services based on a series of intelligence, preference, and aptitude tests. If these counseling services are not available or if you wish to get further evaluation and recommendations, there are numerous approved vocational guidance agencies where batteries of tests are given to help individuals make career selections based on their indicated interests and aptitudes.

The accounting profession itself, through its professional organizations, has also devoted considerable research to the determination of personal traits and aptitudes desirable in accountants. These groups have developed a series of tests that measure aptitude for accounting, and these have been found to be remarkably accurate in predicting whether an individual is likely to do well in accounting courses and, ultimately, in an accounting career. The series includes tests for use in high schools and colleges. These tests emphasize the ability to identify and solve problems. Information concerning the tests can be obtained from the American Institute of Certified Public Accountants, 1211 Avenue of the Americas, New York, New York 10036.

APTITUDES

Aptitudes are natural abilities or the capacity to acquire readily those abilities that enable us to do certain things well or understand a given subject. Accountants should have the following aptitudes:

- A feel for figures
- A sense of orderliness
- An analytical turn of mind
- An appreciation for accuracy
- A healthy curiosity

- Vision and constructive ability
- Determination to carry things through to a conclusion
- Ability to handle mass detail without losing perspective

For most accounting work, a knowledge of higher mathematics, while sometimes helpful, is not essential. However, a feel for figures is vital. Consistently poor grades in arithmetic, algebra, and geometry indicate a disinterest in figures and corresponding lack of ability to use them meaningfully. To accountants, figures have meaning. They instinctively relate them to results and consider them in ratios to and percentages of other figures. When relationships between these figures seem out of line, they want to know why. They are cautious about accepting things at face value and look for underlying reasons behind variations from anticipated results.

Appreciation for accuracy, which stands high among aptitudes accountants should possess, does not relate only to accuracy in figures. Accuracy in word usage and presentation of facts, both orally and in writing, are equally important. Ambiguous terminology or omission of a material fact can cause a financial statement to be misleading, and thus inaccurate, even though all the amounts appearing in the statement may be correct.

Accountants and auditors usually work with data recorded and summarized by others. A single figure on a financial statement or production report may represent hundreds of individual items. An example of this is the number of items that are summarized to arrive at the dollar amount of an inventory shown on the balance sheet of an automobile company having several factories, branches, and warehouses. That figure represents a summary of individual inventories taken at each factory, branch, and warehouse of automobiles ready for sale, partly assembled cars, tires, tubes, parts, and such raw materials as foam rubber for seats and upholstery.

Although it is not the responsibility of the accountant or auditor to take the physical inventory or to price it, it is the responsibility of the controller to formulate procedures to assure an accurate inventory and the responsibility of the public accountant to make sure that the inventory was properly taken, valued, and summarized. You will note that handling such mass detail and directing the work of others require several of the mentioned aptitudes.

PERSONAL CHARACTERISTICS

Professional accountants work at executive levels whether they are engaged in public or private accounting. Many of their personal characteristics, therefore, are common to executives in other occupations.

For those planning to make public accounting a career, it is especially important that they like people and enjoy working with them. The duties of public accounting require its practitioners to meet and work with different people as they go from one client's office to another. Accordingly, they should be able to "size up" people quickly and deal with them effectively. Good leadership ability is very beneficial to accountants because such ability inspires confidence from others. Of course, public accountants must be tactful and present a neat appearance, which creates a good first impression.

Private accountants must possess these same traits, the only difference being that, since they are more likely to be with the same business associates for longer periods, strong ability to meet new people frequently and to evaluate them quickly becomes a less important factor.

There may be a few isolated specializations in accounting where introverts are preferred, but certainly not many. This fact is overlooked by many high school and college guidance counselors. Most successful accountants tend toward extroversion. They are gregarious, self-assured, and somewhat aggressive. Additionally, most have a liking for new, challenging situations; a readiness to innovate and lead; and an interest in working with others. Contrary to the popular misconception, accountants—at least the effective and successful ones—do not prefer secure, unchanging, always predictable assignments. Rather, they are self-starting individuals who are always alert for opportunities to test and improve their professional skills.

CHAPTER 3

EDUCATION

The aptitudes, skills, and attitudes, as well as technical competence that are fundamental to success in professional accounting will develop most effectively during your high school and college education. A college degree with a concentration in accounting has become the norm. Nearly all state boards of accountancy (the licensing agencies for practicing public accountants) require that candidates who sit for the CPA examination must have at least the equivalent of four years of college education. CPAs require the broadest kind of education to understand, analyze, and report on management operations and to recognize problems and propose solutions. This training can be acquired through education programs that lead, ideally, to a graduate degree in accounting or through the curricula offered by professional accounting schools.

In some universities, the accounting program is offered in a school of accountancy; in others, it is provided in the college of business administration. Certain core courses are required. Generally, accounting courses will include financial accounting theory, auditing, taxation, and cost analysis and control. Economics, management, marketing, finance, quantitative methods, and computer technology are included in the business courses comprising a degree program. As mentioned earlier, speaking and writing skills are so important that wherever possible, electives in those subjects should be taken.

HIGH SCHOOL

Today's aspiring professional accountants should be concerned very early in their education with acquiring accounting and business knowledge as well as important interpersonal skills. This training can begin in high school through a college preparatory program. Subjects in the college preparatory course—languages, science, and mathematics—constitute a better foundation for accounting training at collegiate level than do business subjects. Although all required subjects in the curriculum are necessary for a well-rounded background, perhaps the most important one is English. The ability to write and speak well is a plus factor in all walks of life, and the inability to do so is a constant handicap. Courses in mathematics are also important—not because these subjects have a direct relationship to accounting but rather because they serve to develop reasoning ability, accuracy in dealing with facts, and facility in using figures.

COLLEGE

Higher education for accounting can be accomplished in a variety of academic settings—four-year liberal arts colleges, undergraduate schools of business, two-year junior colleges followed by two years in senior college, and undergraduate business or nonbusiness study followed by graduate business school. Appendix B in the back of this book lists United States schools offering courses of study leading to a degree with a major in accounting.

A model educational program drafted by the American Institute of Certified Public Accountants recommends that about half of a student's undergraduate study be devoted to general education subjects. Such nonaccounting subjects as communications, behavioral sciences, economics, and computer science, for example, are considered useful.

Communications. Effective communication, both written and oral, is an indispensible skill of the professional. In every course, the student should be required to demonstrate continuing ability in written communication. Concern is not with literary style but rather with the student's ability to convey the intended message clearly, concisely, and precisely, without errors in grammar, punctuation, or spelling.

Behavioral science. The accounting profession's interest in the behavioral sciences results from accountants' need to understand individual and group behavior, the decision process, and organization theory. Topics of specific interest include authority, learning, motivation, conflict, and innovation. Accountants need to know the process by which individual and organizational decisions are made. And, as members of organizations working with and for other complex organizations, they must understand the formal and informal networks of individuals and groups within organizations, chains of command, fixing of responsibilities, cross loyalties, information flows, and controls.

Economics. An understanding of economics is essential to accountants. For that reason, it is advisable for students to incorporate into their college programs courses in macro- and microeconomics.

Computer science. A basic knowledge of computers—what they are and what they can do—should be a part of any student's general education. Such knowledge is essential for those planning to enter accounting careers. Introductory courses in computer science should be taken during the first or second year in college and should give an understanding of at least one computer system—the functions of its component parts, the general capabilities of the system, and the general terms associated with computer science. Students should develop a working knowledge of at least one computer language sufficient to permit them to program and debug a simple problem.

SPECIFIC ACCOUNTING STUDIES

In recent years, AICPA has noted a growing practice at undergraduate business schools of limiting the number of semester hours a student can devote to any single subject. While this concept lays the groundwork for a broad education covering many disciplines, it should be applied with caution to prevent inadequate accounting training. It is generally accepted that a broad, well-rounded education can be attained through a five-year course of college study, made up of generalized courses such as those outlined, together with a portion of the curriculum devoted specifically to accounting. College students preparing for accounting careers very often do not decide whether to accept employment in private or public accounting until they are approaching graduation. By following a curriculum meeting the most rigid CPA education requirements, they will avoid the possibility of being required to make up deficiencies if they decide to enter public accounting and become certified. The study program AICPA recommends includes four main accounting areas—financial, managerial, taxes, and auditing. The overall objective is to give students an understanding of the functions of accounting and the underlying body of concepts that comprise accounting theory as well as the applications of both to business problems and situations. A discussion of AICPA's proposed accounting curriculum follows.

FINANCIAL ACCOUNTING

Financial reporting theory. This deals with financial accounting measurement, including such areas as the determination of period income, revenue recognition, cost allocation, and the flow of funds. Inventory valuation, depreciation theory, liability recognition, and corporation equity measurement are also included in the study of financial accounting theory. Additionally, an understanding of the fundamentals of accounting would be incomplete without a good knowledge of the means by which accounting data are communicated, and this embraces a study of accounting statements, their form of presentation, and accounting terminology.

Applied financial accounting problems. While is it neither necessary nor desirable to delve into every possible situation that might be encountered in the practice of accounting, certain topics are important to an understanding of the complexities of business and finance.

Contemporary financial accounting issues. Students must learn to understand that accounting is a living, growing discipline, requiring its practitioners to be aware of and involved with the issues of the day. The topic coverage of this segment of the accounting curriculum will change more frequently than other segments.

COST OR MANAGERIAL ACCOUNTING

Cost determination and analysis. This is the study of the measurement and accumulation of costs, including such topics as direct and indirect costs, the rationale behind cost allocation procedures, cost-volume relationships, and the application of burden.

Cost control. This course is intended to help students develop familiarity with the controls that are afforded in the application of cost accounting concepts to the design of information systems. Included here are flexible budgets, responsibility accounting, profit center analysis, and standard costs.

Cost-based decision making. The purpose of this course is to build understanding of how accounting can contribute to decision making and planning. Typical problems covered might involve make-or-buy decisions, product mix, capital budgeting, or inventory planning.

TAXES

Tax theory and considerations. This course helps students to place in perspective the multitude of tax laws, regulations, and administrative and judicial rulings, with a broad appreciation of the tax structure and its role both as a source of revenue and as a device to influence the economy.

Tax problems. In addition to having a broad background in the field of taxes, accountants should be able to apply tax principles to the solution of specific, complex problems involving individuals, corporations, partnerships, trusts, and estates. Only when they understand the interrelationships among these can students develop a sense of the impact of taxes on decision making and planning.

AUDITING

Audit theory and philosophy. Auditing, whether it is done by an independent accountant or an internal auditor, contributes to the reliability of financial and other data. How this is done comprises auditing theory and philosophy, an essential part of an accountant's knowledge. This subject covers such topics as evidence, authorizations, sampling, review of internal control, and arithmetic controls and reconciliations. Also included are the role of independent auditors, their legal responsibilities, their code of ethical conduct, and their standards of reporting, field work, and competence. The role of internal auditors as they function within management organizations also is covered.

Audit problems. As in other areas of accounting, students' understanding of auditing principles is reinforced and expanded by exposure to problems and cases. Subjects covered in this course might include statistical sampling, internal control, and auditing computerized accounting systems as well as the more traditional problems dealing with, for example, the confirmation of receivables, inventory observations, and the fixed asset audit.

Computers and information systems in business. Building on students' earlier exposure to computers, this course explores the strengths and weaknesses of the computer in the business context, develops skills with higher level EDP languages and simulation techniques, and develops understanding of the relative strengths of the human being and the machine in symbiotic human-machine interaction. It also involves the investigation of complex systems, the techniques of analyzing and flowcharting them, the development of basic skills in system and design, and an understanding of the control procedures required.

Although this accounting curriculum is suggested to meet CPA requirements, it is noteworthy that the same education is favored by business organizations for those whom they place in training programs for executive accounting positions and by federal government agencies such as the General Accounting Office and the Internal Revenue Service.

College degrees do not necessarily indicate course content. Some schools grant B.S. (bachelor of science) degrees, others B.A. (bachelor of arts) degrees, and still others B.B.A. (bachelor of business administration) degrees to students following about the same curriculum. The important things to find out are if the school has a good faculty and if it offers a sufficient number of credit hours in accounting and related subjects. Obviously, it is difficult to get an unbiased opinion of a school's faculty. Alumni may be biased as a result of personal experience or school loyalty, and, furthermore, they would have no yardstick by which to make an evaluation unless they had attended more than one school or had some other basis for comparison. On the other hand, the number of semester hours available in all subjects is a matter of record in school catalogs, which can be used as a guide to meeting stated requirements.

GRADUATE STUDY IN ACCOUNTING

Some schools have programs of study leading to an M.B.A. (master of business administration) or M.S. (master of science) degree for graduate work in accounting. These programs require one or two years of study beyond a baccalaureate degree—the length of time depending primarily on the student's undergraduate curriculum. The program would generally be one year for an accounting major and two years for those who did not major in accounting at the undergraduate level.

An undergraduate degree in English or economics with two years of graduate work in accounting is an ideal background for those planning careers in accounting. It is too bad that more liberal arts schools do not point out to their students the opportunities that are available to those following such a program.

On the other hand, there is some question concerning the merit of graduate work in accounting for students who majored in accounting at the undergraduate level, and there is no positive answer that will apply equally to all students. The answer depends to a large extent on the content of the undergraduate curriculum, the character of the graduate program, the scholastic records of the students, and the reasons for considering graduate study. Were their college grades good, and do they have the capacity to benefit from graduate work? Do they plan to teach? Do they think that another degree represents an ''open sesame'' to better employment opportunities? These are a few of the questions that would require answers before a considered opinion could be formed, for in the final analysis, the value of additional schooling must be related to the value of practical experience that could be obtained during the same period of time.

Certainly graduate study is valuable for individuals who have the capacity to benefit from further abstract study. However, a proliferation of undergraduate subjects is not recommended. The student who received a bachelor's degree with an accounting major probably should not take more than nine to twelve semester hours in accounting out of the approximately thirty semester hours required for a fifth-year master's program. Most of the subjects should be in the area of behavioral and management sciences.

GRADUATE STUDY OF LAW

Accounting students planning to specialize in taxation often seek advice concerning the necessity for a law degree. A law degree is not essential for accountants who specialize in taxation. Probably there are more tax specialists who are not lawyers than there are those who are. However, the study of law provides an excellent background for any position in the business field, and it is certainly very desirable for accountants specializing in taxation.

In recent years, there has been a substantial increase in the number of accounting majors who have entered law schools. It is also true that employers' demand for persons having both an accounting and legal background has greatly increased.

A CPA will find a legal background helpful in all phases of tax work. But the income tax law is based on accounting concepts, and therefore a sound background in accounting, including several years of practical experience, appears to be a better foundation for a specialization in tax work than a law degree without such experience.

EVENING CLASSES

What if the aspiring accountant cannot afford to attend college on a full-time basis? Is there another way to gain the necessary knowledge and experience? Probably not one that will provide the high degree of proficiency demanded of accountants today; however, it is possible to obtain an accounting education through evening classes, which allow students to divide their time between work and study. Most colleges offer evening classes; usually, six years of evening study are required to complete the four-year day-school-degree curriculum. Attendance at evening school has both advantages and disadvantages, the latter generally outweighing the former.

Most students who are enrolled in evening courses have little time to spare for anything other than work and study when school is in session. Unless they are unusual, either work or study, or both, may suffer because of time limitations.

The quality of instruction in evening schools varies. At some schools, a major portion of the teaching load is carried by full-time day-school teachers, but at others, part-time teachers predominate. Some part-time teachers, because of their knowledge of the practical aspects of the subjects they are teaching, may be superior to those on the full-time faculty. With others, this may not be the case. It is one thing to know a subject and quite another to be able to teach knowledge of that subject to others. Be sure that the part-time evening program you select is accredited and is preparing well-qualified accountants. You might want to talk to some former students and those currently enrolled in the program to learn more about it.

PART-TIME EMPLOYMENT

Many accounting students who are enrolled in full-time college programs obtain part-time employment with public accounting firms or in the accounting departments of companies. Such experience is held in high regard by business organizations and accounting firms when it comes to selecting personnel to add to their staffs. This part-time work, of course, helps defray college expenses; but beyond that, it provides the beginning accountant with a useful introduction to the type of work accountants do. A job applicant with experience in the accounting field gives evidence of maturity and stability and may be expected to understand the work better than a novice. Often, part-time work with an accounting firm or in the accounting department of a company, begun while in college, leads to a permanent position with that company after graduation.

INTERNSHIP TRAINING

The word *intern* is usually used to describe a graduate medical student undergoing resident training in a hospital. However, the accounting profession has extended its use to describe accounting students taking part in programs that provide them with a short period of practical experience while they are enrolled in college.

Internships in public accounting provide students with valuable diversified experience and often result in employment offers from cooperating firms after graduation.

Internship programs for accounting majors are sponsored by colleges and conducted in cooperation with employers—principally firms of certified public accountants. Students given the privilege of obtaining this training are permitted to drop out of school during their junior or senior year for periods varying from a few weeks to several months, generally during December, January, February, and March. They are employed by cooperating firms and receive salaries only slightly less than those paid to recent graduates. In addition, many cooperating firms pay the cost of transportation from the interns' schools to their offices and return. The months mentioned include the usual peak period of work in most practices, and therefore students experience typical work in public accounting.

It is not uncommon for schools to allow only students having a scholastic average of B or better to take part in internship programs. Setting this minimum gives schools some assurance that interns have the capacity to make up the classroom work they missed while away from school and that they have the capabilities to accept staff assignments with cooperating firms under the supervision of experienced accountants. Students planning to serve an internship should endeavor to take additional courses during their sophomore and junior years in order to carry a lighter schedule during their senior year when they will spend several weeks off campus. The same result could be attained by attending at least one summer session before interning.

Some schools follow the practice of assigning interns to employers while others give each student the opportunity to be interviewed by representatives of cooperating firms and the privilege of accepting any employment offer.

A few schools also sponsor internship programs with industrial concerns. These programs are generally conducted during summer vacation periods. Students who accept positions with cooperating industrial organizations are given the opportunity to work in accounting positions of different types or are assigned to special projects and studies enabling them to get a good idea of the operations of the accounting and administrative departments. It is also quite usual for these industrial internships to result in employment offers after graduation.

CHAPTER 4

PROFESSIONAL CERTIFICATION

The CPA certificate is a measure of entry-level competence in accounting. State boards of accountancy regulate entry requirements into, and the practice of, public accounting. Each state establishes its own education, experience, and other requirements. Certification is achieved by passing the Uniform CPA Examination. This examination is administered in all states, in the District of Columbia, and in the United States territories of Guam, Puerto Rico, and the Virgin Islands.

The CPA examination is given to all candidates who meet the requirements established by the board of accountancy in their state or territory. It stresses not only technical knowledge and its application but also the exercise of good judgment and a comprehension of the professional responsibilities of a CPA. Both theoretical and practical problems in financial and management accounting, auditing, federal income taxation, and business law are included on the examination.

Ideally, the CPA examination is best taken as soon as the requirements for candidacy are met. In addition to preparation in college, there are intensive review courses and self-study programs designed to better prepare candidates for the rigorous two-and-a-half days of tests. The examination, which is given twice a year, consists of four parts. Not all candidates pass all four parts at one sitting.

In many states certification and licensing are one and the same. In a growing number of states, however, the CPA certificate is separate from the license to practice public accounting. In part, this trend is in response to the growing number of accountants employed in private industry. In forty-eight states, CPAs are required to take continuing education courses to maintain their competence. This requirement has principally focused on CPAs in public practice whose independent audit services have great importance to the financial world, investors, banks, and government at all levels. Separation of the certificate from the license facilitates eliminating the continuing education requirement for those CPAs who choose careers in industry, education, or government.

Both CPAs and non-CPAs who are pursuing careers in industry can receive certification denoting special competence in management accounting. The CMA certificate requires that the candidates successfully pass an examination that covers economics, finance, internal and external reporting, electronic data processing, quantitative methods, and managerial accounting.

The certified public accountant credential is an academic achievement which provides a valuable entry to the world of professional accounting. A CPA employed in industry, although not rendering independent auditing services to the public, still retains the right to use the designation CPA, although it is usually in connection with the title of the position held in the company. The *public* in certified public accountant takes on special meaning and importance in a state where the certificate and license are one and the same. It also has particular significance for those CPAs who, after obtaining their licenses to practice, choose to present themselves to the public as being engaged in the practice of public accounting. Let's take a more detailed look at the CPA credential in the remainder of this chapter.

THE CPA CERTIFICATE

What is the meaning of the CPA certificate? How is it obtained? What kind of examination must be passed? What are the education and experience requirements? Who prepares the examination? Who issues the certificate? Is a CPA certificate necessary for a career in accounting?

The CPA certificate is granted by state governmental authorities to accountants who have passed a rigid written examination and met certain education and experience requirements. It gives the holder the right to use the title certified public accountant or the letters CPA and to obtain a license to practice public accounting in the state granting the certificate. Persons other than those who have been granted the CPA certificate are barred by law from using that title or the letters CPA. The fact that states exercise this authority indicates that it is in the public interest to identify competent and responsible accountants who may offer their services to the public and on whose opinions people may rely in connection with investing money, extending credit, and making other financial decisions. The laws of the various states differ as to education and experience requirements, even though all states give candidates the same written CPA examination.

THE CPA EXAMINATION

Accounting is the only profession that has been able to reach an agreement and offer a uniform examination in every state and territory. The Uniform CPA Examination is given twice a year, in May and November. The painstaking procedures for drafting, administering, and grading it have been developed over a period of seventy-five years. The examination is prepared by the Board of Examiners of the American Institute of Certified Public Accountants, which is made up of educators, former members of state boards of accountancy, and practicing public accountants.

The examination consists of four parts:
accounting theory
business law
auditing
accounting practice

The accounting practice examination is divided into two parts and requires a full day; the others require one-half day each. Elaborate precautions are taken not only to make the examination a demanding measure of the candidate's knowledge and ability but also to ensure fairness and objectivity in grading. All states and territories use the institute's grading service to mark candidates' papers in order to assure uniform grading. However, it should be noted that the American Institute of Certified Public Accountants is retained by the board of CPA examiners of each state to perform this service and that it is the state board and not the institute that has the primary responsibility for the examination, the grading, and the issuance of CPA certificates. This is best indicated by the fact that some state boards, operating under their CPA laws and regulations, require candidates to take tests in such subjects as municipal accounting, ethics, economics, and finance, which are not part of the Uniform CPA Examination and which are not prepared or graded by the institute. Furthermore, boards of CPA examiners in some states review and make test checks of the institute's grading before informing candidates of the results.

Changes in the Uniform CPA Examination have been approved by the board of examiners and have received the support of the AICPA Board of Directors and NASBA Board of Directors. These changes will be effective with the May 1994 examination.

1. The examination's structure and time will be:

SECTION	TIME
Financial Accounting & Reporting–Business Enterprises	4 1/2 hrs.
Accounting & Reporting–Taxation, Managerial, and Governmental and Not-for-Profit Organizations	3 1/2 hrs.
Auditing	4 1/2 hrs.
Business Law & Professional Responsibilities	3 hrs.
TOTAL	15 1/2 hrs.

2. The format for each examination's section will be:

FORMAT

SECTION	4-Option Multiple Choice (%)	Other Objective Answer Formats (%)	Free Response (%)
Financial Accounting & Reporting	50–60	20–30	20–30
Accounting & Reporting	50–60	40–50	———
Auditing	50–60	20–30	20–30
Business Law & Professional Responsibilities	50–60	20–30	20–30

The percentages are for that portion of a candidate's grade to be allocated to technical content only.

3. Selected answers to free-response (essay or problem-type) questions will be graded for writing skills.
4. For the examination's financial accounting and reporting and accounting and reporting sections, handheld calculators will be provided to candidates as a part of the examination material.

Essentially, the CPA examination is a test to measure judgement and intelligence in the application of accounting principles, auditing standards, and procedures to practical problems and to evaluate understanding of professional ethics. The examination is no more difficult than similar ones given to entrants in the professions of law and medicine; however, it is true that the number who fail the CPA examination is proportionately somewhat higher.

A number of coaching schools have been established to help persons prepare for the CPA examination. Although these do not pretend to be schools of accountancy, many candidates have found them to be useful in reviewing earlier studies and thus helping to raise examination scores. Correspondence courses also are available to achieve the same purpose. Most efforts to help students on the exam lean heavily on the published questions used in previous exams, with the correct answers. These are available from the AICPA.

Most states give credit for successful completion of two or more parts of the CPA examination, and in these states, candidates are required to retake only the parts they previously failed. A study of examination results showed that a substantial majority of those who have taken the examination have eventually passed all parts.

VALUE OF THE CPA CERTIFICATE

The CPA certificate is evidence of professional status. It is tangible evidence that the holder has met high standards of competence in accounting. Other accountants may have equal ability and some may have far greater knowledge in a particular area than the CPA, but there are few, if any, accounting positions in which the CPA certificate will not add prestige or its value not be recognized.

Those planning to practice public accounting would find their futures limited without a CPA certificate. All partners of firms of certified public accountants must be CPAs or the firm cannot use that designation. In many such firms, staff members cannot advance to top staff positions until they become certified. In some states, the practice of public accounting is not restricted to certified public accountants, but it is nonetheless true that those practicing public accounting without a certificate are working without the advantage of educational achievement and status attained by passing the CPA examination.

Women and men pursuing careers in private accounting may not find the certificate as necessary for advancement to positions of greater responsibility within their own organizations and, in most instances, when seeking employment in another company in the same line of business. There are many top financial positions held by noncertified accountants. But there are times when the holder of a CPA certificate has the edge over the one who does not have the same evidence of ability. When a vacancy at management level occurs for which no understudy is available, it is not unusual for employers in the business field to favor a certified public accountant to fill the position.

Similarly, the certificate is not essential for those employed by government in the accounting area, but here again, CPAs are often preferred over non-CPAs for responsible positions.

EDUCATION REQUIREMENTS

The American Institute of Certified Public Accountants recommends a four-year college course with an accounting major as the minimum educational background for becoming a CPA. There are sixteen states that allow a person with less than a bachelor's degree to sit for the examination and obtain certification. Of those sixteen states, Georgia, North Carolina, Ohio, and Washington allow people to obtain certification with less than a bachelor's degree only if they pass a special written examination prepared under the direction of the board of accountancy that tests their education level. This special exam is required in addition to, not in place of, the Uniform CPA Examination prepared by the AICPA. There are twenty-two states that reduce the experience requirement needed for candidates with more than a bachelor's degree. Some states specify that the degree must have been granted by a college approved by state authorities. To obtain approval, a college must maintain certain teaching standards and offer a program of study for accounting majors similar to the one recommended by the AICPA.

EXPERIENCE REQUIREMENTS

Most states require a period of practical experience in accounting before they will grant a CPA certificate. There is considerable variation between states as to the length and type of experience considered acceptable and whether the experience is a prerequisite to taking the examination or may be obtained later.

Most states require one to three years of public accounting experience before candidates are permitted to take any of the four parts of the examination, but in some instances this experience requirement may be reduced or waived if similar experience has been obtained in the business field or with government agencies. Also, the amount of experience required is sometimes related to the educational background of the candidate.

CHAPTER 5

PUBLIC ACCOUNTING

The first CPA law was enacted in New York in 1896. Fifty years later, there were only about 30,000 certified public accountants in the United States. By the early 1970s, their number had surpassed 140,000. Today, there are over 392,000 CPAs in the country. A significant turning point in this growth arose in the mid-1930s through the federal securities acts. These acts required independent audits of corporations that issued securities to the public. As a consequence, the demand for the services of independent professional accountants accelerated rapidly.

THE PUBLIC ACCOUNTING PROFESSION

The public accountant serves many clients, as opposed to the industry or private accountant who is usually associated with one business entity. The difference between the work of a corporate CPA controller and that of the CPA in public practice is comparable to the role of chief legal counsel in a company and the attorney conducting a private law practice. The entire worktime of the industry CPA is devoted to the demands of one company, although this may extend operationally to multiple divisions or even other companies whose business is part of the larger corporation's organization. The public accountant serves many clients as an objective outsider or in an advisory capacity. The practicing CPA and the industry CPA are responsible for understanding the same body of accounting knowledge. The application, however, varies because there is a difference in the fundamental purpose of the two professional fields of accounting. Earlier in this book the role of the public accountant was described as unique. It is the dual responsibility of serving the client and still being primarily responsible to third parties that creates this uniqueness.

The public accounting profession grew, therefore, out of the need to provide audits conducted by persons not associated with the management of the company being audited. In fact, fairly extensive ethical rules have evolved that delineate the relationship a public accountant must maintain in order to be viewed as independent of the company being audited. These rules on independence in general require that a CPA not have a financial interest or participate in any way as a member of the company's management during the period covered by the financial statements that the independent CPA is auditing. Because of these and other ethical responsibilities, the audit function was assumed by public accounting firms organized to provide audits on a fee basis and staffed by persons who were not employees of any of the companies they audited.

Public accounting firms grew in number as quickly as did the number of new CPAs. By 1970, there were more than fifteen thousand public accounting firms in the country. In 1990,the American Institute of CPAs included more than forty-three thousand firms that ranged from sole practitioners to small, medium, and large CPA firms. The largest public accounting firms practice internationally, employ thousands of professional staff, have hundreds of partners, and may maintain offices in foreign countries and most major cities in the United States. As you would expect, as a firm grows in size, so too does its ability to offer a wider range of specialized services to the public. There are some very large single office firms in the United States that can provide a wide range of services, but geography will play a greater role in their interest in serving clients outside a specific region. The media and business community commonly refer to public accounting firms in relation to their geographic service range. The descriptions generally follow the titles of local, regional, national, or international firms.

Public accounting services fall into three broad and overlapping classifications: auditing, taxation, and management services. General practitioners perform all these services for their clients, and auditing may represent the greater part of their work. However, whether conducting a general practice or specializing in one of these areas, public accountants will find their work varied and stimulating, never narrow or restrictive.

In fact, variety is one of the principal attractions of professional work. Public accountants not only render different types of services to clients but also serve clients in a wide variety of businesses. As public accountants go from one client's office to another, they obtain a knowledge of systems and procedures; of management problems; and of operations, products, and services of businesses both small and large. They gain a familiarity with the unique or unusual accounting features applicable to different kinds of organizations—the accounting for depletion in mining companies; the plant and property accounts of public utilities; the retail inventory method used by department stores; appropriation and fund accounting followed by institutions and governmental bodies; and the important accounting and legal distinction between principal and income in accounting for estates and trusts. They learn what makes business tick.

The work of public accountants is carried out in clients' offices, either locally or in other cities or countries. Their duties bring them in contact with people having varied backgrounds and interest, and accountants learn to meet people, evaluate them, and work with them effectively. Public accounting experience represents a continuing education. Even the beginner will find that this broad experience will develop self-confidence and assurance—ingredients necessary to success in any field.

PRACTITIONERS

Public accounting practices are conducted by individuals, by partnerships, and by professional corporations. Partnerships are referred to as firms rather than companies even though the firm name may include the word *company*. The *company* designation in such cases means "and other partner(s)" and does not indicate that the firm is incorporated.

Both individual practitioners and small firms may employ other accountants as members of their professional staffs, but it is quite common for individual practitioners to conduct their practices without a staff or with a relatively small one. When their work expands and a larger staff is required, they often find it expedient to take in one or more partners.

In size, public accounting practices range from the individual practitioner without staff assistants to the international CPA firms having several thousand staff members and offices in the major cities throughout the world.

Professional services vary according to the needs of clients and the capabilities of the practitioner. All practitioners are expected to follow high professional standards of workmanship, conduct, and ethics. Staff members receive wages and benefits based on the size of the firm, the type of practice, and the services offered by the firm with which they become associated. Some of the distinguishing features of firms according to size are given here to assist you in evaluating the various opportunities in public accounting.

Firms are generally classified as small, medium, and large. Small firms employ fewer than twenty staff members, medium-size firms employ from twenty to a hundred, and large firms employ a hundred or more. Accurate statistics are not available concerning the number of practitioners classified by size, but there are far more individual practitioners and small firms than medium-sized and large ones. Some of the large firms are described as national because they have offices in the major cities throughout the country, and a few are referred to as international because they also maintain offices in foreign countries.

Small Firms

Individual practitioners and small firms render valuable and necessary professional services to that large segment of the economy known as small business. They serve clients as general practitioners, examining their accounts, preparing their tax returns, and consulting with them on financial and business problems. These practitioners usually have a diversified clientele, but there are some whose clients are predominantly in one kind of business, such as the garment industry, finance companies, or automobile agencies.

The operations of many small businesses are not of sufficient size or complexity to warrant the employment of a full-time controller or even a full-time bookkeeper. In such cases, clients look to the individual practitioner, or a partner of the firm retained, to provide the financial advice and counsel that the controller would normally supply in a larger organization.

Small practitioners also do write-ups and prepare monthly financial statements. *Write-ups* is a term used by public accountants to describe either a complete bookkeeping service or making the necessary month-end adjustments of bookkeeping records prepared by clerks or bookkeepers. Monthly statements that have been reviewed by a CPA are especially desirable for small companies because it is not always possible to establish internal checks and controls in such companies in order to safeguard cash and prevent other losses resulting from stealing and falsification of records. In connection with monthly accounting and bookkeeping services, financial statements are usually prepared, and reports on operations and financial conditions are customarily supplied to managements.

Medium-size Firms

Medium-size public accounting firms, as might be expected, have some of the characteristics of both small and large firms. Their clientele usually consists of a large number of small clients and a few large ones engaged in a variety of business enterprises. But, like small firms, some medium-size ones also tend to specialize in services for certain kinds of businesses. Many of these firms have offices at more than one location, principally to serve their large clients having several branches.

Large Firms

Large firms, although fewer in number, tend to be more widely known by name to the financial community and the public than other practitioners because their accountant's opinion often referred to as the accountant's certificate, appears on most of the annual reports sent to stockholders by large publicly owned corporations. They have offices located in a number of cities in the United States, and some of them also have foreign offices.

The clientele of large firms, with few exceptions, is greatly diversified, covering all kinds of business, institutions, and organizations, both large and small. Partners of these firms and key members of their staffs, although qualified to handle any type of engagement, tend to become specialists in certain businesses, such as public utilities, mining, publishing, department stores, financial institutions, and municipalities. Most large firms also have separate departments specializing in taxation and management services.

THE PUBLIC ACCOUNTANT'S WORK

Of the three major fields in which public accountants work—auditing, taxation, and management services—public accountants are most widely known for their work as auditors. In fact, clients usually refer to the public accountants they retain as "our auditors" or "our outside auditors,' the latter to distinguish them from employees in their own auditing departments. But to persons who are not accountants, the work of the auditor is not well understood. Perhaps the following will clear up some of the misconceptions concerning auditing work.

Auditing

Contrary to popular belief, auditing is not merely a matter of checking figures or of verifying the correctness of bookkeeping entries. The purpose of an audit is to substantiate the validity of financial statements or other data being audited. When auditing financial statements, auditors must review contracts, agreements, bond indentures, minutes of boards of directors' meetings, and various other documents to ascertain that all matters affecting the financial condition of the client have been recorded on the books, and they must also determine that the entries are in accordance with generally accepted accounting principles. They must correspond with debtors and creditors and banks to confirm the accuracy of data appearing on the books. They must supervise or observe the taking of physical inventories or satisfy themselves by other means that inventory quantities are accurate and that they are extended, footed, and summarized correctly.

They must do many other things in connection with an audit, but their examinations are usually limited to tests. The extent of such tests depends on the system of internal check in effect in the client's organization—that is to say, the extent to which the work of the client's employees is divided in order to minimize the possibility of honest error or fraud in the accounts. To make an effective audit, the auditors must study the system of internal check and control. Such work requires knowledge, experience, and judgement, and it is a far cry from merely checking figures and bookkeeping entries. A knowledge of computerized accounting systems is now required for auditing.

Many people are of the opinion that the main reason public accountants are engaged to audit books is to detect misappropriation of funds and other frauds, but this is only incidental to the basic purpose of an audit. And widespread management fraud may be difficult to uncover.

Another erroneous popular belief is that the CPA's report or certificate on a financial statement means that each amount on the statement is precisely accurate and that other auditors would arrive at identical amounts. Of course, this is not so. Accounting is not an exact science, and the financial statements are those of management. The auditor does not guarantee their total accuracy. Many complex questions affecting financial position and operating results are not subject to definitive answers. In some instances, principles can be formulated to arrive at greater uniformity in accounting statements, but the answers to many questions are a matter of professional opinion based on the facts surrounding each case, and we all know that opinions differ. Doctors, for example, do not always diagnose ailments the same or prescribe the same medicine to persons having the same illness. Certainly no one will ever be able to say that the net income of a business for an arbitrary length of time is precisely correct. But the independent public accountant, after completion of an audit, is able to express an opinion that the figures may be accepted for all practical purposes and fairly represent the financial picture of the company.

In sum, it is the auditor's responsibility to test the propriety of financial statements. Checking goes well beyond the basic review of mathematical computations. Financial statements can't simply be added up and presumed to "tell the whole story." They are really a complex combination of facts, judgements, and even estimates. To audit financial statements, a CPA follows established auditing procedures, which are supplemented by the auditor's experience and judgement. An audit engagement is planned in advance, based on a knowledge of the type of business involved and a preliminary examination of the accounting system and records. Normally the company's internal accountants prepare the financial statements and accompanying footnotes for the auditor's examination and opinion.

One of the exciting facets of public accounting is that each audit engagement may involve different types of enterprises and, with each, there is a need to develop a working knowledge of that industry or type of business. The greater the knowledge, the better able the auditor is to evaluate the data provided by management. Irregularities are also easier to uncover. An important area in the audit is the company's internal control system. This is management's way of maintaining its records and protecting its assets. Company policy serves to curb dishonesty and keep the system orderly and uniform. Typically, internal control is carefully apportioned among different departments or persons, each of whom is responsible for receiving money, recording receipts, depositing funds, reconciling bank statements, or paying company bills. The auditor must take a very careful look at this internal system to determine if it is, in fact, working as it is designed to. Weaknesses in the system lead the auditor to revise the audit plan and examine further if the problems arise in an area where material amounts of money may be involved or basic policies are not being observed by company employees.

The auditor does not test or review every transaction, except in the most unusual circumstances. Sampling techniques are now used to test the accuracy of the transactions and the accounting system. It is necessary to compare orders and receipts with company records to confirm that the transactions took place. Important corporate documents, such as leases and contracts, are reviewed. If questions arise, the auditor expands the search and examination to obtain further evidence and assurances. All the standards and rules in the world do not tell the auditor what experience and judgement can tell. Auditors develop a "nose" for something that is not right. Auditing is a skill that is sharpened and refined by on-the-job training.

Upon completion of the testing procedures, the auditor reaches a conclusion that is to become the auditor's report. There are two general conclusions that an auditor can reach. If the financial statements are fairly presented in conformity with generally accepted accounting principles, the auditor will affix the firm's name to the report. This results in a clean opinion. If, however, some aspect of the financial information presented is unsatisfactory, the auditor considers another form of report. The auditor may qualify the opinion by stating specifically what issue or item is not presented satisfactorily. The other alternative is either to disclaim an opinion expressing no conclusions because of the magnitude of the concerns—or to express an adverse opinion. In the latter case, the auditor is saying that the financial statements are actually misleading. It is rare for a report to be issued with an adverse opinion.

It would be difficult to overemphasize the importance of the independent CPA's opinion on financial statements. The opinions of CPAs are accepted as authoritative by investors, stockholders, creditors, and management not only because of their professional competence but also because of their objectivity and professional independence. These opinions are of fundamental importance to investors, shareholders, banks, credit grantors, underwriters of security issues, and others. In fact, much of the great expansion of the American economy through the granting of credit and equity financing is in significant measure made possible by the confidence that can be placed in auditors' opinions. Thus, the work that goes into the analysis of an enterprise's financial condition and operating results is both exacting and comprehensive. This necessarily calls for the highest professional skill and judgement.

The Securities and Exchange Commission, an agency of the United States government, requires that financial statements submitted to it for registration in connection with the sale of securities be certified by independent public or independent certified public accountants. Bankers generally request prospective borrowers to submit certified financial statements before making loans. Security holders expect to receive at least annual certified financial statements from corporations in which they have investments to assist them in deciding whether to retain, increase, or dispose of their investments. Security analysts use them in evaluating security portfolios of customers of stock brokerage firms.

Those responsible for the funds of institutional and nonprofit organizations realize the desirability of submitting financial statements bearing the opinion of independent public accountants to those interested, as an assurance that the funds have been properly administered and accounted for. Trustees appointed by the court in bankruptcy cases find the services of independent public accountants to be of great value. Prudence dictates the need for an examination and report from independent public accountants on the financial condition of a business being purchased or sold.

However, professional accountants' auditing services are not limited to the examination of financial statements. It is not uncommon for them to be called on to verify or determine the proper settlements made, or to be made, under the provisions of patent, royalty, and compensation agreements, contracts, and leases. For example, lease rental may be based on a percentage of sales or receipts; royalties may be payable upon sales or profits of one of several products; bonuses may be computed upon net income, excluding certain types of expenses. Accountants' auditing abilities also are used in assembling facts and making studies for management in connection with contemplated mergers, consolidations, and liquidations. Arbitrators appointed to settle financial disputes turn to independent public accountants to prepare studies upon which to judge the merits of the representation of the parties involved.

Proprietors or managers, especially of small and medium-size organizations, look to public accountants to evaluate the work of their bookkeepers and accountants while making an audit of their accounts and to recommend changes in procedures that will result in greater efficiency or more effective internal control. Also, those responsible for the conduct of business enterprises, both large and small, consult with their public accountants as well as their lawyers before entering into contracts having financial implications.

Taxation

Certified public accountants have played a major role in taxation for many years. This broad field includes federal, state, and local income taxes; franchise and personal property taxes; foreign taxes; and estate planning. Naturally, the majority of accounting work in this area is in income tax, since the determination of taxable income is basically a matter of accounting. Here, accountants prepare federal, state, and local income tax returns; consult on tax problems; and plan tax programs. They also represent clients before taxing authorities and advise them concerning the tax effects of proposed transactions.

In estate planning, accountants generally work with lawyers, banks, certified life underwriters, and insurance companies, although it is not unusual for a plan to be initiated by an accountant. All public accountants need a good working knowledge of income tax laws and regulations, and some become tax specialists, devoting all their time to tax work. The larger firms of certified public accountants generally have tax departments composed of specialists who handle the more complex tax problems and review returns prepared by members of the audit staff.

Management Services

Automation and the computer have made business managers more alert and responsive to improving management controls and making changes to attain greater efficiency. Accountants, through basic training and experience, are particularly well qualified to assist them in this area. As a result, the expansion of accountants' work in management services has been phenomenal.

These services include a review, survey, or study of accounting and management functions of clients to ascertain that accounting and statistical information is readily available to and is being used effectively by management as a device to regulate and control operations; that an adequate system of internal control is maintained to guard against losses through theft or waste; that accounting and clerical costs are kept at a minimum, consonant with objectives, through use of the most efficient machine methods and by elimination of unnecessary, wasteful, or duplicate record keeping and reports; and that the activities of departments and operational units are coordinated. Management services also include the installation, modification, or complete revision of accounting systems, procedures, and methods necessary to give effect to recommendations resulting from such surveys and studies.

Public accountants, in the normal course of audit engagements and as a by-product of carrying out the usual audit procedures, are in an excellent position to offer constructive suggestions and recommendations in these areas, and they are always on the alert to do so. However, suggestions and recommendations resulting from an audit engagement are bound to be somewhat limited because such an engagement is not designed primarily as a management survey. Naturally, a review, survey, or study of management functions, such as those mentioned, requires time and knowledge and generally constitutes a separate engagement to which public accountants specializing in management services are assigned.

Most large public accounting firms have separate departments operated by specialists who devote all of their time to management services. Some of these specialists have training in management science and system design and work in such fields as operations research, plant layout, work measurement, and production control. Those working in such fields usually hold master's degrees in management, engineering, or mathematics. However, for most accountants in management services, several years in auditing, training in making management surveys and systems, and a good knowledge of business machines, including electronic equipment, are adequate.

STAFF CLASSIFICATIONS

Staff classification is the term used to describe positions on the professional staff of public accounting firms. They indicate the responsibility area in which the staff member works. The most commonly used staff classifications are junior, semisenior, senior, and supervisor. Some of the larger firms also use one or more additional classifications, such as manager or principal. The responsibilities of staff members in each of these classifications are discussed below.

Juniors

New accounting graduates enter firms as juniors and work under the direction of semisenior and senior accountants. The type of work juniors are assigned varies according to the size and nature of the engagement. They may be assigned to assist in evaluating the effectiveness of internal control or in auditing cash, customers' accounts, inventories, or income and expense accounts. Their work often requires the review of contracts, payrolls, and other confidential matters. At times, their duties may seem to be routine in nature, but juniors seldom find them uninteresting because they must constantly be on the alert, use imagination, and exercise judgement. They advance through the ranks as they gain experience and show ability to assume more responsible work. The normal time required for juniors to advance to semisenior level is about one year, but some beginners attain that rank in a shorter period, and some may take more than two years to achieve promotion.

Semiseniors

The duties of semiseniors do not differ materially from those of junior accountants, except that semiseniors are assigned to more complex and responsible work and require less supervision. Semiseniors may also be placed in charge of small engagements or important phases of large engagements, working under the general supervision of seniors or supervisors. In such cases, semiseniors are responsible for and direct the work of junior accountants. They assist in preparing financial reports and in drafting letters and memoranda for submission to clients concerning such matters as internal control procedures. After development in this classification, the next step is to the rank of senior accountant. One or two years is the usual time required for this advancement.

Seniors

Staff members at this level are directly responsible for the conduct of engagements, working under the general supervision of managers or partners. Their duties include planning the work to be undertaken; assigning the proper grade of accountants to the various tasks; directing and reviewing the work of all assistants; consulting with officials and employees of clients relative to matters that arise in connection with an examination; and preparing financial statements, reports, and tax returns. The abilities of seniors vary. In firms using the supervisor classification, seniors having qualifications to be in charge of examinations of multicompany operations (large companies having several subsidiaries and plants located throughout the country) are generally classified as supervisors. Whether they are classified as seniors or supervisors, these accountants coordinate the work of staff assistants at all locations and have less qualified seniors under their general direction.

Seniors and supervisors assume heavy responsibilities, and at this point their advancement depends not only on technical competence but also on whether they possess administrative and executive ability. Most accountants with sound technical knowledge and training will attain senior or supervisor rank, but some go no further because they lack qualifications for top-management-level work. Those who possess such qualifications will advance to manager level within a reasonable time in large firms and will be in line for partnerships in smaller firms.

Supervisors

As indicated, in some firms this classification is used to designate senior accountants with superior ability. In other firms not using the manager classification, their responsibilities are similar to those in the manager rank.

Managers

The term *assistant partner* describes quite accurately the duties and responsibilities of managers. They have general supervision over a number of engagements, reviewing with seniors and supervisors the audit programs, personnel requirements, and plans for each engagement before work is undertaken, and they are expected to develop their staff assistants. During the course of engagements, they review the progress of the examination and discuss with seniors, supervisors, and top officials of client organizations matters of a controversial nature requiring solution. They edit financial statements and reports prepared by seniors and supervisors before they are typed and submitted to partners for final review and signature. In short, they are responsible for the administrative as well as the technical aspects of all engagements coming under their direction. Individuals having these responsibilities are likely to become partners of their firms. They compare in stature to partners in small firms and treasurers and controllers in large business organizations.

Partners

In small firms, accountants who meet with distinction all the demands of their profession usually become partners. As partners, they carry the ultimate responsibility for the quality of service to clients and for the administration of the firm. They contribute to the formulation of policies and the solution of problems affecting not only the firm but often the accounting profession as a whole. They share all the rewards and satisfactions of influential positions in the modern business world.

PROFESSIONAL DEVELOPMENT

A firm has an important investment in the professional progress of each person it employs. All personnel are given every assistance and encouragement to develop their capabilities to the fullest, and throughout their careers, no matter what firm they work for, most accountants will receive some form of advanced training and professional development enhancement.

The basic introductory training for new staff members often is an intensive course simulating actual audit experience. It is designed to bridge the gap between academic study and practice as well as to familiarize the newcomer with the firm's special methods and procedures. These courses, usually held during the summer months, give excellent preparation for the kind of work accountants encounter during their first year on the job. They are taught by women and men in the firm who have outstanding ability and expertise. The classes usually are restricted in size in order to permit individual instruction.

By far, the most important part of an accountant's professional training takes place on the job, under the close supervision of seasoned staff members and through actual job experiences. Job assignments cannot, of course, be used solely as a tool for training, but they are planned, as far as is possible, to assure diversified experience at the highest level of which a staff member is currently capable. In a sense, on-the-job training never ends because each new engagement presents new and different problems for staff members at all levels and for partners and individual practitioners as well. Well-planned, on-the-job training for young staff accountants is important for sound and rapid development, and most firms make a point of giving them this kind of training by assigning them to diversified work for different types of business organizations.

On-the-job training is supplemented by participation in a series of formal courses and seminars on such matters as taxes and current developments. Seminars often are conducted on a conference basis, allowing a free and informal exchange of ideas and experiences and giving staff members practice in the productive give-and-take of the conference table.

At the senior level in larger firms, there are often regional meetings that include carefully planned programs designed to welcome and initiate senior accountants to their new duties. At the managerial level, there are likely to be national meetings to discuss important professional subjects.

Other aids to professional development include the articles appearing in a firm's publications, special memoranda and publications concerning developments of current interest prepared by various committees of the firm, and the extensive facilities of the firm's library and research departments. Additionally, in order to encourage participation in professional activities, CPA firms usually pay staff members' annual dues in the American Institute of Certified Public Accountants and in a state CPA society.

OPPORTUNITIES IN PUBLIC ACCOUNTING

Opportunities for those with several years' experience in public accounting are almost unlimited. They can remain in public accounting, accept positions in business or government, or plan to teach accounting.

Most staff members do not consider leaving public accounting until they become CPAs; however, shortly thereafter, it is not unusual for them to reappraise their future prospects and decide what course to take.

Many stay in public accounting with their employers, advancing through the ranks to top staff positions, either on the general practice staff or in a specialization such as taxation or management consulting. A high percentage of those who remain later become partners of the firms employing them.

Public accounting is essentially a personal service that gives staff members ample opportunity to demonstrate their abilities and adequate scope to use them to the fullest extent. Advancement in public accounting is quite consistently based on ability rather than on length of service, and staff members having partnership potential can look forward to becoming partners in ten to fifteen years.

While some staff members prefer to cast their lots with their present employers, others start their own practices. As in other professions, the going is rough for the first year or two while the firm is young, but after that, income will increase in relation to the competence of the practitioner. The ever-growing recognition of the services that CPAs can render to small business organizations indicates that new practices can be successfully developed.

Generally, those staying in public accounting, either with their present employers or in their own practices, do as well financially as those who leave to accept other positions. However, there are a number who leave because public accounting requires out-of-town travel and, particularly during the busy season, long working hours and pressure in meeting deadlines. Moreover, similar to doctors and lawyers, public accountants in responsible positions are always on call when clients require their services.

As indicated, public accounting provides an excellent background for positions of responsibility in the business field. A survey several years ago showed that one-fourth of the top executives of American industry were CPAs. Business recognizes the value of broad diversified experience coupled with the objectivity developed in public accounting, and clients often turn to the firms of certified public accountants they retain for assistance in filling such important accounting positions as treasurer, controller, or assistant controller. Furthermore, it is not uncommon for clients to ask specifically for the staff accountants assigned to their engagements to fill such vacancies. Pubilc accounting firms willingly cooperate with clients in this way since placement of staff members can be expected to result in cementing client relationships.

However, those who enter public accounting as a stepping-stone to positions in business should plan to stay in public accounting for at least five years—preferably, seven or eight years—before making a change. During this period, they should become certified public accountants, for it is accountants with such backgrounds who receive the most desirable offers. Staff members rarely leave public accounting to accept positions with business or industry unless such positions offer substantially greater compensation immediately in addition to good future advancement possibilities.

There are several thousand accounting and auditing positions in the federal government and many more in state and municipal governments. These governments are constantly seeking personnel with public accounting training. The staff of the Internal Revenue Service includes many CPAs who work as agents, investigators, and bank examiners. Additional employment opportunities exist with the Securities and Exchange Commission and the General Accounting Office at the federal level and with such local-level government agencies as school boards and sewer districts.

The teaching profession presents interesting opportunities to CPAs as faculty members in college accounting departments. Some young people who plan careers in teaching enter public accounting to gain practical experience before accepting a faculty appointment. Students graduating from colleges and universities with degrees in accounting are expected to exceed fifty thousand annually during the next few years. In college and university teaching, those having minimum training and experience may receive the rank of instructor without tenure; advancement and permanent faculty status depend on further education and experience.

CHAPTER 6

MANAGEMENT ACCOUNTING

Financial accounting and management accounting are not two distinct subjects. They both need to be viewed as parts of accounting. The body of accounting knowledge is the same as the accounting principles used for financial reporting. It is the purpose and application that will distinguish the management accountant from the public accounting professional. In simplest terms, management plans, organizes, and controls. These activities require many complex and interrelated functions and are carried on simultaneously in a company. Each of these activities requires management to make ongoing decisions, and that is the role of the management accountant.

THE MANAGEMENT ACCOUNTING PROFESSION

Eric Kohler's widely used *Dictionary for Accountants* defines *management accounting* as:

...accounting designed for or adapted to the needs of information and control at the various administrative levels of an organization. The term has no precise coverage but is used generally to refer to the extensions of internal reporting for the design and submission of which a corporation controller is responsible. Repetitive reports on performance involving both product quantities and dollars, special reports covering operational areas undergoing change, or proposed for reorganization, and reports of investigations of malfunctioning or suspected inefficiencies are illustrative of the manifold activities in which the present-day controller, frequently with the assistance of the public accountant, is expected to engage. Emphasis is often given to prompt, authoritative, and complete reports that can lead to and even induce management decision making. An illustration of management accounting is *activity accounting.*

A CPA employed as a management accountant is responsible for developing, producing, and analyzing data useful for decision making. These data also include information that will be reported to interested parties outside the company. Today, the number of management accountants who are CPAs is rising rapidly. Over 40 percent of the CPAs who are members of the AICPA and state CPA societies are employed in business and industry. Within a few years, the majority of members in these professional organizations will be from industry. The CPA credential is important because of the great value placed on the financial management function.

Management plans are directed toward achieving certain financial results. The company's resources must be wisely allocated and its human resources most efficiently directed. In addition, management must stand ready for and capable of prompt access to credit and capital markets so it can finance needed expansions and research and development and so it can cover short-term financial needs. Financial reporting to investors, banks and other lending institutions, and governmental agencies must be acceptable and ready should management need to seek outside funds.

The accounting field, then, comprises more similarities than differences if we are talking about accounting standards. In some respects, accounting principles are of primary concern to management accountants since it is their financial statements that are submitted to independent auditors for examination. The outside auditors determine if management has, in their opinion, complied with the established accounting principles. Both groups of professional accountants are responsible for a thorough knowledge of accounting. Both have responsibilities regarding reporting of information and judgments to third parties who will rely on this information to make investment and other decisions.

There are literally thousands of large and small businesses in manufacturing, selling, importing, exporting, and service fields that might
be prospective employers for management accountants, also known as
private accountants. Then, too, there are different types of nonprofit
institutions—colleges, hospitals, research foundations, and charitable
organizations such as the American Red Cross and the USO. The variety
of opportunities seems endless.

Although the private accounting field is made up of organizations of
all kinds and sizes, the accounting used in every business is basically
the same. On the surface, this does not always seem to be the case,
because accounting records, methods, and procedures of organizations
in different lines of business, of different sizes, are dissimilar. For
example, the accounting records of banks are unlike those of other
organizations and, of course, the accounting methods and procedures
for large companies are more complex than for small ones. But these
things do not change the basic fact that accounting fundamentals and
principles are the same in all organizations. This is significant because
it means that an education in accounting provides the background
necessary for accounting in any organization.

THE TYPE OF WORK

The nature of the work of private, or management, accountants differs
somewhat from that of public accountants. Private accountants are
concerned primarily with managment and administrative problems.
Their duties tend more to the constructive and practical aspects of
accounting while those of public accountants generally relate more to
the analytical and technical side.

Not many years ago, accountants in the business field were looked
upon as recorders of financial history, having as their major responsibility the submission of financial data to management concerning past
operations. But this has changed. Now, accountants are not only responsible for reporting on past operations but also for interpreting them for
management and for forecasting future financial results and capital
requirements. They have become an integral part of the management

team. The top positions in private accounting require broad-gauge individuals because little can happen in any organization that does not involve money and financial planning.

There are many important positions for management accountants. The top ones in the accounting area generally carry the title of vice-president–finance, controller, treasurer, or a combination of these titles. Others include assistant controller, budget director, chief accountant, general auditor, and tax manager. Management accountants also find that their training and experience provide an excellent background to advance to positions that are not strictly accounting in character.

Obviously, beginning accountants do not begin in these top positions immediately after graduation from college. A beginner might gain experience by starting as a member of the general accounting department of a company, working as an assistant to the chief accountant, or as the head of a section of the department such as the accounts receivable or accounts payable division. Beginning accountants might also start as members of cost departments, tax departments, audit departments, or with methods and procedures groups. In some organizations, new accountants are known as trainees and are rotated through several departments for periods varying from a few months to a year or more before receiving permanent assignments. Where beginners start and the nature of their work will depend on openings available, personal interests, and the indoctrination procedure of their employers.

KINDS OF POSITIONS

A detailed description of the numerous positions in private accounting would be impossible within this book. However, a good idea of the kinds of positions open to accountants in this field can be gained by a brief description of the more important accounting functions.

The responsibility for controlling accounting functions and the titles given to those having that responsibility vary in different organizations according to the size of the business, the method of operation, and the philosophy of management. In some of the larger companies, the vice-president–finance is the chief financial officer, and the treasurer and controller report to him or her. In companies not having a vice-president–finance, the treasurer is usually the top accounting and financial officer. In others having both a treasurer and controller, the controller is the major accounting executive, and the treasurer's responsibilities are limited to finance matters. Similarly, some organizations use the title assistant controller or plant accountant to designate the person in charge of accounting at a production unit while other companies use the title chief accountant for that purpose. Titles are not important to this discussion. The functions, rather than the titles given to those responsible for the functions, are considered here.

Vice-President–Finance

This position is usually, but not always, filled by an individual trained in accounting. The vice-president–finance is the chief financial officer, reporting directly to the president and assuming overall responsibility for the accounting and finance functions for which the controller and treasurer are directly responsible. The vice-president–finance would probably be the financial advisor for the company in connection with any acquisitions or merger negotiations. Other responsibilities of this position would include capital acquisition, credit policies, and cash management.

Controller

The controller (same as comptroller) is the chief accounting executive and is responsible for all phases of general accounting, cost accounting, budgets, methods and procedures, taxes, and often for internal auditing. The controller is expected to keep informed concerning all external developments having a bearing on the financial operations of the company. A person in this position must be alert to favorable and unfavorable trends in costs and sales and must work intimately with the heads of production and sales departments in order to correlate the activities of these departments and to assure the most effective use of capital and an adequate profit margin. The job, as indicated, is extremely varied, requiring a firm grasp of business, a sound knowledge of accounting, and the ability to deal effectively with people.

The Financial Executive Institute outlines the functions of the controller as follows:

- Planning for control. To establish, coordinate, and administer, as an integral part of management, an adequate plan for the control of operations. Such a plan would provide to the extent required in the business, profit planning, programs for capital investing and financing, sales forecasts, expense budgets and cost standards, together with the necessary procedures to effectuate the plan.
- Reporting and interpreting. To compare performance with operating plans and standards and to report and interpret the results of operations to all levels of management and to the owners of the business. This function includes the formulation of accounting policy, the coordination of systems and procedures, plus the preparation of operating data and special reports as required.
- Evaluating and consulting. To consult with all segments of management responsible for policy or action concerning any phase of the operation of the business as it relates to the attainment of objectives and the effectiveness of policies, organization structure, and procedures.
- Tax administration. To establish and administer tax policies and procedures.
- Government reporting. To supervise or coordinate the preparation of reports of government agencies.
- Protection of assets. To assure protection for the assets of the business through internal control and internal auditing; to assure proper insurance coverage.
- Economic appraisal. To appraise economic and social forces and government influences and to interpret their effect on the business.

Treasurer

In organizations not having a vice-president–finance or a controller, the treasurer is the chief financial officer assuming the responsibilities mentioned above. The basic functions of a treasurer in organizations also having a controller are arranging for meeting capital needs; handling corporate investments; managing relations with creditors, stockholders, and bankers; and administering insurance coverage and credit policies and collections. This position may also represent a crucial step for those aspiring to chief financial officer. It functions within the inner circle of top management.

Assistant Controller

As the name implies, persons having this title may act as general assistants to the controller or may relieve the controller of direct responsibilities in certain management and administrative areas. An assistant controller may work at the same location as the controller or may be the accounting head at a subsidiary company, plant, or product division. Some large companies having far-flung operations have several assistant controllers. The assistant controller has the same responsibility in areas coming under the jurisdiction of the office as the controller has for the entire company. The personal requirements for holding such a position are similar to those needed for controllership.

Plant Accountant

This title is often used to designate the accountant in charge of accounting at a particular production unit. The plant accountant would usually report directly either to the controller or an assistant controller. In some instances, the duties and responsibilities of plant accountants are the same as those of assistant controllers. The fact that plant is part of the title generally indicates that the person in this position is responsible for accounting at a production unit, and this usually requires a thorough knowledge of manufacturing processes and cost accounting as well as general accounting.

Chief Accountant

The person in charge of a large accounting department or several departments making up an accounting unit is often given the title chief accountant. The chief accountant generally supervises and coordinates such accounting sections as the cashier's department and payroll department and is responsible for the preparation of financial and operating statements.

The chief accountant works under the general direction of an assistant controller or plant accountant in large organizations or the controller in smaller ones. A good technical knowledge of accounting and practical experience are requisites for this job. Also, since the chief accountant is at the hub of accounting where data are collected, recorded, summarized, and then disseminated, that person must have a good understanding of all interdepartmental and intercompany relationships in order to direct assistants.

Chief Cost Accountant

The head of a cost accounting department or large cost unit is usually known as the chief cost accountant.

Cost accounting is an extremely important segment of accounting. It deals with the allocation of the basic elements of costs—labor, material, and overhead—to products and to units of operations. It also deals with the recording and summarization of such data and its interpretation for use by management. Business in a competitive economy requires detailed cost information to operate profitably. Good cost accounting is the best defense against excessive costs.

Cost accountants must have a comprehensive knowledge of cost accounting, a good understanding of general accounting, and a detailed knowledge of the production and manufacturing processes relative to the products on which they are collecting cost data. Furthermore, cost accountants must be constantly on the alert to investigate variations from standards, to revise procedures in order to establish more accurate costs, and to obtain cost information in the most economical way. The good cost accountant should possess imagination, be meticulous concerning detail, and have a good sense of proportion.

The designation *cost accountant* is often used erroneously to describe any person working on cost records in a cost department. Most cost departments have many cost clerks but few cost accountants.

General Auditor

The general auditor is responsible for all auditing functions of a company and reports directly to the president, the chairman of the finance committee, the vice-president–finance, or the controller, depending on the size of the business and the line of authority established. Auditing functions are generally carried out by a group of well-qualified auditors, known as internal auditors, whose work is similar in some respects to that of public accountants. However, auditing departments in some organizations are composed mainly of audit clerks whose duties are largely routine, requiring little if any accounting knowledge. This discussion does not include the work of audit clerks, although they do come under the direction of the general auditor.

What is internal auditing? The Institute of Internal Auditors states that ''basically, internal auditing is a control that is concerned with the examination and appraisal of other controls—in seeing that the assets of a business are properly protected and accounted for, that current transactions are promptly and completely recorded, that faulty, inefficient, or fraudulent operations are revealed, and that the business is adequately protected against waste, fraud, and loss.''

Some internal auditors do considerable traveling. They examine branches, division offices, and subsidiaries that may be located nearby, in other parts of the country, or even abroad. The financial audits they conduct are generally of a more detailed nature than those made by public accountants for large companies. The internal auditor's work includes a careful review of procedures to determine that company policy is being followed and to ascertain that financial data are being supplied to the head office on a uniform basis throughout the company. This uniformity is essential for accurate comparisons and evaluations of the operations of one unit with another, and it also facilitates the preparation of combined or consolidated balance sheets and operating statements for the company as a whole. The most desirable background for this work is accounting study at the college level supplemented by public accounting experience or special training in the employer's methods, procedures, and policies.

Internal auditors are frequently required to prepare comprehensive written reports covering their examinations. These reports are used by management and are usually reviewed by the firm of certified public accountants retained by the company. Public accountants can generally limit the scope of their examinations as a result of the work of internal auditors.

Tax Specialist

Taxes assessed by federal, state, and local governments are one of the major costs of operating a business. Many corporations, therefore, have tax departments composed of specialists in tax matters. These specialists establish procedures to control tax aspects of day-to-day transactions and are called on to determine the tax consequences of new projects under consideration by management. They prepare tax returns or supervise their preparation and represent their companies in contacts with taxing authorities.

Tax specialists need a good background in accounting and taxation. They must have an understanding of tax laws and regulations applicable to the various kinds of corporate taxes, such as social security, unemployment insurance, sales and use, federal and state income, franchise, and property taxes. Some employers believe that these specialists should have a law degree in addition to a degree in accounting.

Methods and Procedures

This function has taken on added significance in recent years, and most larger companies have separate departments composed of accountants and industrial engineers who devote all their time to studying methods and procedures in an endeavor to reduce operating and administrative costs, improve communications relating to financial information, establish effective management controls, and improve financial reporting. In other companies, this function is not departmentalized, and internal auditors are often given the responsibility for this work. In small organizations, this function would be the direct responsibility of the controller.

Methods-and-procedures work in the business field corresponds to the work of management specialists in public accounting. Those working in this area should have training in management science and knowledge of electronic computers as well as an accounting or general business background.

Budgetary Control

Budgets are forecasts that provide a basis for management planning, operating controls, and performance appraisal. Managements of most large concerns and many medium-sized and small ones want to know well in advance how their companies will make out financially, assuming that certain sales volumes can be attained. Income and expense budgets are the source of this information since they are usually prepared for a fiscal year in advance and represent estimated standards or goals of performance by which efficiency of operations can be measured. However, if budgets are to be meaningful, the estimates used therein must be realistic and reasonably accurate—not a matter of mere guesswork. Therefore, the preparation of budgets is placed in the hands of persons trained in this work.

The budget director heads a staff that prepares an income and expense budget and obtains data relating to anticipated sales, revenue, and other income and to the estimated costs of producing that volume of sales and the amount of selling and administrative expenses involved. The staff obtains this information in sufficient detail to enable it to prepare an estimated income account for the company as a whole and estimated operating statements for each department and production unit separately. Before these estimates are summarized, they are considered and appraised critically, both in relation to past performance and to anticipated future occurrences such as variations in economic trends. It is not unusual to have all estimates reviewed and approved by a budget committee composed of the controller, sales manager, and production manager before final budgets are prepared.

In addition to income and expense budgets, budgets are often prepared with reference to capital expenditures, cash, and inventories. Budgets of all kinds provide bases for comparing actual performance with predetermined standards. The budget director and staff make these comparisons and investigate variations.

This brief explanation of the duties and responsibilities of the budget department's staff may tend to oversimplify by omitting specific reference to the many involved problems that arise in this work. The work is not routine. The budget director and staff assistants should be well versed in accounting, have a good grasp of all phases of their employer's business, and have the ability to work effectively with others.

Credit and Collection

The extension of credit to customers and the collection of amounts due from them are not accounting functions in a strict sense. Yet some knowledge of accounting is very desirable, if not essential, because anyone responsible for granting credit must know how to analyze financial statements and related data in order to form sound judgments. People trained in accounting have the background to do this, and therefore they are often selected for credit work.

A company's credit and collection practices can have great effect on the availability of working capital as well as on customer relations. An accountant who understands the need for maintaining a fine balance, tuned to the individual company's particular financial condition, can help establish policies that will maximize cash flow without jeopardizing future sales.

TRAINING PROGRAMS

The broad objective of training programs is to accelerate the development of personnel for supervisory and executive positions. The more specific objectives are to train employees in the methods, procedures, organizational structure, and management policies of their employers. Methods followed to attain these objectives differ. Some companies do not have formal training procedures while others have programs for employees at various experience levels.

In general, only larger companies provide formal training programs for accountants, and these usually consist of planned on-the-job experience coupled with rotational work assignments. Extensive orientation and formal training programs of the classroom variety, conducted during regular working hours, are the exception; but there are a few industrial companies and financial institutions that conduct such programs. It is noteworthy, although not surprising, that most companies having well-defined training practices also follow a promotion-from-within policy.

There is no such thing as a typical training program for beginners in business organizations. Each company develops its own program, taking into account the educational background of the trainees, the work they are best equipped to undertake at the time of employment, and the general area for which they are to be trained.

Because of the variety of positions in the business field open to those having some accounting training, companies employ not only graduates who majored in accounting but also those who majored in other subjects—for example, business administration, mathematics, management, and liberal arts. However, graduates who did not specialize in accounting but plan to work in the financial area are expected to study accounting through attendance at evening schools or by taking correspondence courses. A number of companies conduct evening classes in accounting and related subjects for their trainees, and even those who specialized in accounting while at college are expected to attend programs that are devoted primarily to the application of company methods and procedures to general accounting practices. Some companies arrange with local schools to provide evening classes for their beginners. In the final analysis, a substantial knowledge of accounting is apparently considered essential for advancement in the financial end of almost all business organizations.

Planned on-the-job training for graduates having different specializations indicates that an accounting major would be a logical choice for initial assignments to the cost or general accounting departments while a mathematics major might be assigned to the statistical research department and a management major to the methods and procedures department.

To attain training objectives through rotational work assignments, beginners are transferred from one department to another, spending a few months in each department, where they gain a basic knowledge of the work carried out in each department and the problems inherent in such work. This initial program may cover a period of two years or more and include periods in the cost, general accounting, budget, credit, methods and procedures, and audit departments. During their experience in these different areas, beginners are counseled and appraised by those responsible for their training, and at the termination of this program they will be given positions, which, based upon their individual performances during the training period, they are best equipped to undertake.

In many organizations, training does not stop there. Other methods are followed for greater development of individuals as they gain experience and move up the ladder. These methods vary from special evening classes, seminars, and group meetings concerning specific areas conducted by the employers to executive training programs offered by colleges, continuing education programs given by the National Association of Accountants, state CPA societies, and self-study programs.

In companies where well-defined training programs are not provided, beginners usually are employed for particular jobs, and training is obtained from their immediate supervisors. There is nothing wrong with this tutorial type of training if the supervisors are good teachers and the beginners are employed with the intention of grooming them for advancement to supervisory responsibilities. Unquestionably, more beginners start careers in business with companies not offering formal training programs than with companies where formal training programs are provided.

OPPORTUNITIES

Greater opportunities now exist in the private or management accounting field than ever before. Several factors contribute to this: the expansion of the economy, the cost-price squeeze requiring ever-increasing efficiency, electronic equipment providing a means of processing vast amounts of data upon which management decisions can be made, the greater dependence of business on management science, and the continuing shortage of capable young people entering the accounting field.

Accountants are at the hub of business. Information concerning sales, marketing, production, and all other aspects of operations flow to the chief financial officer for summarization and interpretation. Having this overall knowledge of the business, the individual in this position is quite often the logical choice to be president, and the number selected to fill the president's seat has been on the increase during recent years. Certainly all accountants do not become presidents or even controllers of their companies, but the fact that the chief executive officer's post is opening up more to accounting-trained people is encouraging and is a further indication of the important role accountants are now playing in management affairs.

Capable beginners will have no difficulty in obtaining desirable positions in private accounting. The number of openings has increased not only as a result of the general expansion of business but also because many new positions have been created through the increased use of budgets and the application of computer technology and management science to business operations. In today's market, beginners can advance to more responsible positions in accordance with their capabilities.

Many beginners stay with their first employers, advancing through the ranks to important positions in the financial area. Some, after gaining experience, leave to accept more responsible or challenging positions with other companies, and others leave to establish their own businesses in management consulting or to join firms of management consultants. However, opportunities for management accountants are not limited to positions in the financial area, and a number of those who started in accounting use their background and experience as a stepping-stone to responsible positions outside that field in such areas as production and sales.

CHAPTER 7

GOVERNMENTAL AND INSTITUTIONAL ACCOUNTING

Public sector and not-for-profit institutions impact, in some way, every citizen in the country. In terms of the dollars that are earmarked for social programs and with regard to the numbers of people dependent on smooth operation of such programs, there is little question that each of us is very concerned about the financial reporting and controls of these organizations. Government spending and the taxes we are all so aware of are regular news items. Behind the news are thousands of dedicated accountants and auditors assisting in investigations to determine compliance with policies and regulations as well as other essential accounting functions. Government waste will be a continuing concern for American taxpayers. Not-for-profit institutions are all around us to provide needed services, including medical research, education, and various cultural and arts organizations. The viability and credibility of these institutions requires the same accounting talents and administrative judgments as the corporate sphere. The career opportunities are there for the accountant challenged by these important responsibilities.

Elected or appointed officials are responsible for determining how well programs are working and if they are meeting the goals for which they were established. The dollars provided by taxpayers or contributors must be spent efficiently. CPAs and other accountants in government and not-for-profit institutions assemble and analyze the data needed to help evaluate these programs.

The federal government employs over 43,300 professional accountants and auditors, about 2,200 of whom are hired each year at the entry levels. In these trainee positions, beginning accountants are closely supervised. As they gain experience, the accountants are given more complex assignments and greater responsibility. Promotions and increased salaries occur as responsibilities increase. The agencies with the largest number of jobs are the departments of the Army (4,100), Navy (2,250), and Air Force (1,950); the Department of Health and Human Services (1,250); the Department of Agriculture (1,240); the Treasury Department (1,225); and the departments of Energy and Transportation (680 each).

Federal accountants are very much in the mainstream of all government activities, and more and more, accountants are participating actively in management decision making. Government agencies must have accurate data in meaningful form for both evaluating the financial results of their activities and planning for the future. Government accounting teams provide the financial services needed to keep agency operations on a firm basis. Some of the job duties of government accountants are:

- consulting with program officials on financial results of their operations
- arranging appropriate financial operations for program objectives
- communicating management's requirements to government organizations and contractors
- coordinating activities between and within agencies

Some of the federal government departments and agencies having need for accountants and auditors are discussed below.

Department of Interior accountants perform such functions as auditing the accounts of concessionaires operating in the national park system or accounting for the government's royalty share from the production of leased minerals. Some accounting positions in this department require a considerable amount of travel.

Federal Power Commission accountants examine books and records of electric, utility, and gas transmission companies throughout the

United States in order to provide reliable financial information that the commission uses to regulate these industries.

The Treasury Department's Bureau of Accountants has a wide range of accounting and auditing positions. Accountants in this bureau examine financial statements from surety companies; do investment accounting for government trust funds; and maintain a system of central accounting and reporting for the government as a whole.

Interstate Commerce Commission accountants and auditors hold challenging positions in the field of transportation. They prescribe and administer uniform systems of accounts for carriers; examine carriers' accounts and operations to assure compliance with accounting rules and regulations; and examine carrier financial reports filed with the ICC.

The General Accounting Office employs high-quality accounting graduates in auditor positions concerned with financial and management audits. They take part in audits of the departments, agencies, and corporations of the federal government and audit private corporations having government contracts. The federal government is involved in almost every known economic activity, thus the variety and scope of assignments provide unusual breadth of experience for GAO auditors. There are even opportunities for overseas assignments in Europe or the Far East.

Other government accounting positions can be found in any of the following:

Air Force Audit Agency
Federal Highway Administration
National Credit Union Administration
Federal Home Loan Bank Board
Internal Revenue Service

INTERNAL REVENUE SERVICE

The Internal Revenue Service (IRS) is the arm of government responsible for the collection of billions of dollars in taxes. The IRS hardly needs an introduction because almost everyone is familiar with the revenue agent in connection with income taxes.

Accounting graduates are hired by the Internal Revenue Service as trainee revenue agents and internal auditors. IRS agents in approximately nine hundred cities around the country work with corporate executives, accountants, attorneys, business managers, and taxpayers. They examine accounting records and investigate other sources required to determine federal tax liabilities. As IRS agents are given ample opportunity for advancement and professional development through working on progressively difficult cases, supplemented by advanced training in tax law and regulations, they gain valuable experience and greater expertise in resolving complex tax issues. There are opportunities to move into specialized fields such as fraud investigation, internal audit, and evaluation of taxpayers' appeals.

Opportunities in this career field are good. Approximately 2,255 new agents are hired each year at the entry levels. Newly appointed agents enter a training program that prepares them for promotion up to the full-performance level. Supervisory and executive development is also provided for selected agents who demonstrate potential for such positions. A very substantial portion of the top executive positions in the various IRS offices throughout the country are held by persons who began their careers as agents.

The tax auditor talks with taxpayers in the office and corresponds with them to identify and explain tax issues. Beginners in these positions enter a six-month training program consisting of classroom instruction in income tax law, auditing techniques, taxpayer relations, and other subjects. They also receive on-the-job training under the guidance of an experienced tax auditor.

REQUIREMENTS

The general entry requirements for accountants and auditors in the federal government are four full years of study in an accredited college or university that satisfy the requirements for a bachelor's degree and include twenty-four semester hours, or the equivalent, in accounting or auditing subjects. Four years of professional accounting experience, a combination of experience and education, or certification as a certified public accountant also meets federal requirements. For auditor positions in the General Accounting Office, at least six hours of accounting and superior academic achievement will qualify, with a major in business administration, engineering, mathematics, statistics, computer science, economics, management, or finance.

GS-5 Requirements

Four full years of study in an accredited college or university that met all of that institution's requirements for a bachelor's or higher degree with a major in accounting; or

Four full years of study in an accredited college or university that satisfied the requirements for a bachelor's degree and included or was supplemented by twenty-four semester hours in accounting or auditing subjects (up to six semester hours of the twenty-four may be in business law); or

Four years of accounting or auditing experience or a combination of education and experience fully equivalent to four years of study as described above, which included one of the following:

- Twenty-four semester hours in accounting or auditing subjects (up to six semester hours may be in business law); or
- Certification as a certified public accountant or certified internal auditor obtained through written examination. (The certificate number and date and place of issuance must be shown on your application); or
- Recognized professional stature in accounting based on successful experience in a variety of highly responsible accounting positions and significant documented contributions to the accounting profession through publications, leadership in professional accounting organizations, development of new methods, or comparable achievements.

GS-7 Requirements

The same requirements for GS-5 plus at least one year of professional accounting or auditing experience; or one year of graduate study in accounting or related fields, such as business administration, finance, or controllership; or any time-equivalent combination of experience with graduate study; or

Completion of all requirements for a bachelor's degree (including course requirements) as described for GS-5 and qualification for superior academic achievement; or twelve months of student trainee experience in accounting in a work-study curriculum; or

Completion of required twenty-four semester hours in accounting and sufficient experience to qualify for GS-5 plus one year of technical experience equivalent to grade GS-5 or higher.

EMPLOYMENT AND SALARIES

Practically all civilian positions in the federal government come under the jurisdiction of the United States Civil Service Commission, and, consequently, employees are protected against losing their jobs through changes in political administrations. The commission usually requires successful completion of a written qualifying test to obtain employment; however, for accountants, the test is waived if the applicant is a four-year college graduate with twenty-four semester hours in accounting and directly related subjects.

Accounting applicants receive a notice of rating once their application forms are evaluated; the rating indicates eligibility for hire. Additionally, they are given a numerical score based on their qualifications. Applicants are ranked in a register, along with other eligible candidates, in the order of their numerical scores.

Newly graduated junior accountants and auditors with no experience would probably be hired at a salary of about $16,305 (GS-5) annually. Accountants with a four-year degree and a superior academic record receive a starting salary of about $20,195 (GS-7) annually. An accountant with a master's degree or a bachelor's degree and two years of professional accounting or auditing experience qualifies for a starting salary of about $22,000. Promotions are based on ability and length of service, and federal government development programs give employees an opportunity to expand their abilities and move into higher level positions. Accountants' salaries in the federal government averaged nearly $35,650 in 1987.

As an employer, the government encourages involvement in professional associations like the American Institute of Certified Public Accountants, the National Accounting Association, and also the American Accounting Association.

Information about openings for accountants can be obtained by writing to the United States Office of Personnel Management, Washington, D.C., or by contacting the local Federal Job Information Center in your area. Trained professionals in these offices will mail you the appropriate job announcements, application forms, and pamphlets.

STATE AND MUNICIPAL GOVERNMENTS

State governments are also made up of many departments and agencies, and they likewise need accountants for a wide range of accounting and auditing work. Positions with state governments are similar in many instances to those with the federal government and include bank examiners, tax auditors, insurance department auditors, unemployment insurance auditors and investigators, and accountants for the state controller's office, public work programs, state-operated institutions, and state-owned and operated business organizations. Information about accounting positions with your state can be obtained by addressing a letter to the particular department, or departments, at the state capital. For example, write to the state banking department relative to a position as a bank examiner or to the department of taxation concerning a position as tax auditor. If your state has a civil service commission, information about various openings can be obtained from it.

The accounting requirements of a municipality will depend on the size of the community and the services it provides. Some municipalities operate utilities and transportation companies, impose income taxes, support hospitals and colleges as well as elementary and secondary schools, and carry on many other activities, all requiring accounting controls and hence accountants and auditors.

CHAPTER 8

ACCOUNTING EDUCATOR

THE TEACHING PROFESSION

The tremendous demand for accounting graduates has put a strain on many colleges and universities. Accounting departments and colleges of business administration are aggressively recruiting faculty to meet this demand on both the undergraduate and graduate levels. CPAs are sought for these positions where the required academic credentials can also be met. Universities are establishing schools of professional accountancy, and the American Institute of CPAs is recommending a program of 150 hours of college education in order to take the CPA examination. In addition to the AICPA, the National Association of State Boards of Accountancy, the American Accounting Association, and the Federation of Schools of Accountancy have all endorsed the proposition of requiring 150 hours to qualify for the CPA examination. These organizations hold that with the explosion of knowledge, a person entering the profession needs more accounting studies. Currently, 11 states have passed legislation requiring 150 hours of higher education for certification.

It is common for accounting educators to begin their careers as instructors. With the required advanced experience and education, they expect eventually to be promoted to professor. Teaching skills are certainly a key prerequisite to success in this field. In addition, writing and research are expected of faculty members and are important considerations in promotions and salary increases. Participation in professional activities in accounting education organizations, the AICPA, and the state CPA societies are also viewed highly. Community involvement in public service projects is also encouraged. Accounting educators receive experience in the world of public accounting through faculty internships, working directly on the staff of a CPA firm, or through conducting research on subjects involving public accounting or management accounting.

CHARACTERISTICS AND
REQUIREMENTS FOR TEACHERS

Although students seldom make decisions to teach accounting until after they receive a baccalaureate degree with an accounting major, they should be aware of the opportunities in this area. Of course not everyone is cut out to be a teacher, but those having an interest in teaching should not pass over too quickly the possibilities it offers. It presents many advantages—associations, surroundings, prestige, and the gratification that can come only from helping others develop their potential. Decisions to teach are usually based on a combination of factors, including high scholastic attainment during college, a liking for research and study, encouragement from professors to work for a Ph.D., an increasing awareness of the breadth of accounting and the many unsolved problems facing the profession, an inborn desire to help others, an aptitude for teaching, and a desire to work in a collegiate atmosphere.

Not all decisions to teach are made while students are attending college. Sometimes they are made after students have been in the business field for several years. During that period, perhaps, they taught in evening schools or in industry programs that provided the impetus to enter the teaching profession. Of course, business experience is helpful, and time in the business field will not be wasted. On the other hand, coming to a decision after several years in the business world generally means that individuals will have to give up good-paying positions to return to school, and because of this, many potentially good teachers unfortunately decide against making the immediate sacrifice to satisfy long-range desires. As indicated, business experience for accounting teachers is very desirable, but those who decide on a teaching career while in school can obtain such experience during summer vacations and at other times without monetary sacrifice.

In college teaching, education below the Ph.D. level is a limiting factor, and for a teacher of accounting, both a Ph.D. and a CPA certificate are desirable. A master's degree is usually the minimum requirement for appointment to the rank of assistant professor or associate professor, and a terminal degree (Ph.D. or equivalent) is required for a full professorship. Although many colleges of business administration now consider a master's degree plus the CPA certificate as equivalent to a terminal degree, the number is decreasing. Therefore, a doctorate should be the goal for those planning a teaching career.

FINANCING AN EDUCATION

Financing an education is usually a factor in preparing for a teaching career. However, high scholastic attainment in undergraduate work generally opens the doors to scholarship aid at the master's-degree level, and for those planning a teaching career, even more aid is available for doctoral candidates. Furthermore, many doing graduate work are able to obtain part-time positions as laboratory assistants and instructors to help defray the cost of their advanced education.

Scholarship help is offered by business organizations and public accounting firms. The American Accounting Association also has a fellowship program in accountancy which has for its purpose "to increase the supply of qualified teachers of accountancy." Fellowships are awarded under this program to assist individuals in furthering their preparation, through doctoral studies, for teaching in colleges and universities. Special government loans are also available to those who plan to teach.

TEACHING WORK LOADS

Fixed hours of work for teachers are usually considerably less than for their counterparts in the business field. In large schools of business administration, teachers are generally required to conduct classes from nine to twelve hours a week. Class preparation time requires about twice that many hours unless, of course, the teacher has more than one class in the same subject. There is considerable flexibility in a teacher's schedule; classes may be arranged for mornings, afternoons, or evenings, and class preparation can be done at convenient times. Because of this latitude in scheduling, a number of accounting teachers conduct small public accounting practices or have other business interests that not only supplement their incomes but bring them face to face with practical business problems.

Do not assume that teachers have an easy job. They don't. To advance in rank they are expected to do research and publish the results, to serve on departmental committees, and to keep current with accounting literature and changes taking place in both the accounting and teaching professions.

In addition to moving up through the ranks from instructor to assistant professor, associate professor, and full professor, there are opportunities for a teacher with administrative ability to become department chairperson, assistant dean, and dean. Some go even further.

Considerable prestige has always been attached to positions on college faculties, but this increased even more after former President John F. Kennedy appointed a number of educators to important posts in the federal government. Business organizations during the past few years have been employing many more educators than previously and also engaging the services of faculty members to conduct special research projects.

Those interested in foreign service will find numerous opportunities for permanent assignments in foreign lands and also for some special assignments of less than a year's duration. With the rapid expansion of international trade, such opportunities should expand.

CHAPTER 9

EMPLOYMENT TRENDS AND SALARIES

In 1989, the number of accounting graduates was 57,000. Estimates are that 37 percent of accounting graduates with bachelor's degrees and 53 percent of those with master's degrees of the 1989 graduating class were hired by public accounting firms. The remaining graduates found positions in private industry, government, nonprofit organizations, or education.

A question often asked by students is how vulnerable accounting positions are when the economy slows or there is the effect of a recession. Most companies respond by answering that they have a continuing need for technical and management personnel and that in "tighter" times, financial planning and control become even more critical to the continued operation of the company. Well-trained professional staff members are sought even when the job market looks bleak for other management functions.

Compensation varies by geographical region of the country, and salary information is only meaningful when it deals with positions held by persons with similar education and training. It is, however, desirable for you to evaluate the range of entry-level salaries that exists for new accountants. As you measure the time and cost of your education as well as your personal aptitudes and interests, the relationship of salary and earning power is something you will want to consider carefully.

Recent forecasts indicate that the number of master's degrees in accounting is lower than was projected from previous years. The rising cost of an additional year of college may be a major factor affecting students' decisions to delay their graduate educations. Notwithstanding this factor, the number of students with master's degrees in accounting is expected to grow at a higher rate than those with bachelor's degrees, which means that more graduates will be upgrading their skills. The percentage of women represented among accounting graduates has also increased from 39 percent in 1981 to 49 percent in 1989.

All of these indicators suggest that, in spite of some hesitation due perhaps to the economy, the accounting field is expected to grow in competitiveness and quality as well as in quantity in the next few years.

The figures in the compensation data chart on page 85 have been compiled from hiring statistics in 1990. An effort has been made to avoid extremes and be as representative as possible. It is helpful to remember that comparative costs of living in different parts of the country and the laws of supply and demand play important roles in determining actual offers made in specific cities in the United States.

Starting salaries for accounting graduates who have the qualifications sought by employers compare favorably with those paid to people entering any other profession and are higher than many. Of course, some students will receive higher offers, and others will accept less. Students will find that scholastic achievement is considered important by those employing accountants and that it will have a bearing on the number of offers they receive and the amount of salary they are offered.

During college job interviews, graduating seniors often ask about the possibilities for increased compensation as they gain experience and what the income prospects are in the various accounting fields for those who reach the top rungs of the ladder. Of course, these questions can be answered only in a general way.

Increases in compensation follow demonstration of ability and willingness to accept responsibility. In preceding chapters, you have read how advancement is made through the ranks and the possibilities accountants have to move ahead not only vertically in accounting positions but also in the related fields of production and management. In public accounting, because of the nature of the work, individual ability can readily be displayed, and an individual can move forward rapidly based strictly on merit. This is also true in industrial and business organizations where definite promotion practices are followed. Therefore, it

Professional Compensation Data/1990

	Annual Compensation ($000)		
	20TH PERCENTILE	**MEDIAN**	**80TH PERCENTILE**
Public Accounting			
Entry (<1 year)	20	24	29
Staff (1-3 years)	25	28	32
Senior (3-6 years)	27	32	38
Manager (6-9 years)	32	40	50
Partner**	37	49	65
Financial Accounting			
Credit Analysis			
Entry (<1 year)	N/A	N/A	N/A
Staff (1-3 years)	19	24	25
Senior (3-6 years)	21	28	32
Manager (6-9 years)	28	32	42
Director	31	38	48
Financial Analysis			
Entry (<1 year)	22	25	38
Staff (1-3 years)	24	28	33
Senior (3-6 years)	28	33	41
Manager (6-9 years)	33	41	49
Director	39	49	62
Cash Management			
Entry (<1 year)	N/A	N/A	N/A
Staff (1-3 years)	22	25	28
Senior (3-6 years)	28	35	45
Manager (6-9 years)	34	42	51
Director	37	50	67
Lending Officer	22	30	41
Treasurer	41	52	65
Chief Financial Officer	54	67	86
Private Accounting			
Cost Accounting			
Entry (<1 year)	N/A	N/A	N/A
Staff (1-3 years)	22	26	31
Senior (3-6 years)	27	32	38
Manager (6-9 years)	30	36	43
Director	36	43	54
Edp Auditing			
(Entry <1 year)	N/A	N/A	N/A
Staff (1-3 years)	20	25	29
Senior (3-6 years)	31	37	42
Manager (6-9 years)	37	41	48
Director	41	49	58

| | Annual Compensation ($000) | | |
	20TH PERCENTILE	MEDIAN	80TH PERCENTILE
Private Accounting (*cont.*)			
General Accounting			
Entry (<1 year)	19	22	29
Staff (1-3 years)	21	25	29
Senior (3-6 years)	25	30	36
Manager (6-9 years)	29	37	44
Director	33	43	56
Internal Auditing			
Entry (<1 year)	20	24	28
Staff (1-3 years)	23	27	31
Senior (3-6 years)	27	31	36
Manager (6-9 years)	31	38	45
Director	38	47	60
Tax Accounting			
Entry (<1 year)	N/A	N/A	N/A
Staff (1-3 years)	23	27	31
Senior (3-6 years)	28	35	42
Manager (6-9 years)	32	41	50
Director	41	51	65
Management Consulting**			
Entry (<1 year)	N/A	N/A	N/A
Staff (1-3 years)	21	26	31
Senior (3-6 years)	26	31	39
Manager (6-9 years)	30	39	49
Assistant Controller	34	43	54
Vice President	54	67	84

Data compiled by Source Finance Salary Survey, 1990.

follows that the possibilities for reasonably rapid compensation increments for those in accounting are good. The incomes of individual practitioners and partners of public accounting firms are related to the size and character of their practices.

Starting salaries for teachers of accounting in colleges and universities cannot readily be compared with those paid to accountants in other areas for several reasons, including the fact that usually the only teaching position open to bachelor's-level individuals is that of graduate assistant on a part-time basis while studying for an advanced degree; inexperienced beginners in the teaching profession who work on a full-time basis generally hold a doctorate (Ph.D.) or are working on a doctoral dissertation and have completed one or more years of study over that required for a master's degree; and salaries for teachers are often stated on a nine-months' college-year basis.

Salary scales at large universities are substantially higher than those of smaller schools, and salaries for teachers in schools of business administration are generally higher than the average salaries for all teachers in a college or university. Furthermore, when comparing teachers' salaries with those paid to accountants in industry, public accounting, and government, keep in mind that teachers' salaries are computed on a nine-month basis and that faculty members may also receive additional income as consultants to business, from public accounting practice, from royalties on publications, or for special research. Some also can earn additional income from teaching during the remaining three months of the year.

As discussed in chapter 7, accountants and auditors in entry-level positions earn from $16,305 to $20,195 per year (GS-5 to GS-7). A rating system based on specific qualifications determines the grade level of newly hired accountants. Advancement to higher grade levels and salaries is relatively rapid, and in such settings as the Internal Revenue Service, agents usually move up within three years from trainee levels to advanced positions paying from $29,891 to $38,855 (GS-11). A smaller percentage achieve salaries in the $35,825 to $65,444 range (GS-12 to GS-14). Federal salaries are adjusted periodically to remain comparable to those in the private sector.

CHAPTER 10

CAREER PLANNING

Pick up any major newspaper and turn to the classified business advertisements. Look for the heading for accounting jobs. Good times or bad, there always appears to be a definite need for trained professional accountants. The ads, however, only indicate there are positions available. As you examine the ads more closely, you will notice that the qualifications vary considerably, as does the experience desired. At certain levels, a CPA certificate is not sought. In other positions, computer experience is required. Sometimes a particular industry specialization is wanted. Since you are not looking for that "right" position yet, don't try to develop your career plan from the jobs currently advertised. Many positions are recruited without advertising, and your career path is best set through meeting the requirements of the many CPA firms and corporations that will seek your skills upon graduation from college.

DEVELOPING A PLAN

Planning for career development puts you in control of your professional life and gives you a better chance to match aptitude, interest, and finances with goals. We each have different personality traits, work habits, and timetables for what we hope to accomplish. In this book, we have explored the accounting field. We looked at public accounting practice, management accounting, governmental and institutional accounting, and accounting education. It is hoped that planning and achieving your career goals will be easier now that you have gained some additional insight into the various fields of accounting. You have really taken the first important step toward success in professional accounting. Now it is important to carry your thinking forward and build a clear definition of each of the skills required and set a reasonable path to follow to acquire those skills.

Understanding the Field

A few simple rules can be helpful in maximizing your career development potential. First, be sure you understand the field of accounting. Continue to examine the various positions within the field and the training required. Talk with professionals employed in those positions. Don't miss an opportunity to hear professionals speaking about what their jobs involve. Often state CPA societies and other professional organizations sponsor career days and conferences for students. Look for these opportunities. Sometimes you can identify a trade show on computers or business topics that is open to the public or acccessible for a token fee. Meeting business professionals and staying close to the state-of-the-art technology that accountants are regularly exposed to in their work will keep you in step with the times. Make these opportunities happen.

Establishing Goals

Second, establish your goals. Make them realistic and talk with others about them. Be specific so there is something definite to shoot for. There's always time to change the game plan slightly as your interests or ambitions change. Stay abreast of where you are in your career plan. Be mindful that our society is in the midst of another major explosion in technology that will have major implications for the gathering of information and how it will be used. The first computers seem archaic by today's standards, but they came on the scene only a short time ago. Don't make the mistake of following your game plan so closely that you get left in the Dark Ages! Set your plan of action in motion and review your educational and training progress on a regular basis. If you accept and understand that a professional accountant simply needs more than technical skills to reach the top rungs of the profession, your career planning efforts will be rewarded. Career planning requires imagination, perception, and sensitivity to other people. Plan now and you are well on your way to achieving your goals.

Strangely enough, increased employment opportunities have not made it easier for college graduates to make job decisions. When they must make a choice and they have several offers from which to choose, many graduating accountants begin to analyze their futures more carefully. They are not interested in just any jobs. They want career jobs— jobs offering challenge, advancement, opportunities, and a feeling of accomplishment. Unfortunately, many college seniors have no better than a vague idea concerning the nature of the work, duties, responsibilities, and demands that are inherent in different accounting positions. Even with such knowledge, selecting the right job is not easy; but the decision is an important one. Getting started in the wrong field or in the wrong job during the early development period usually results in a waste of precious time during which valuable experience could have been gained.

College students realize this but seldom do anything about it prior to the time campus interviews commence. Then, during the months preceding graduation when time is at a premium, they spend many hours having interviews on campus, indiscriminately, with representatives from public accounting firms and companies engaged in widely different enterprises, trying to determine what kinds of positions are open to them and which ones offer the best opportunities. Students could save a great deal of time and be more effective during college interviews if they looked into these things prior to their last year in college and decided upon, at least, their general areas of interest.

Organizations are not all alike, and accountants seeking positions with them should give serious study to the question of which ones are best suited to their interests and capabilities. If you are enrolled in a college accounting program, you should seek out information and advice from counselors and teachers regarding the differences among industries, government agencies, and accounting firms—what they offer and what they expect of newcomers to their staffs.

Another good way to learn more about the profession is to obtain some practical experience in both public and private accounting through summer and part-time employment during school. More of these jobs are available than in the past, but applications for jobs should be made well in advance of the desired starting date.

The opinions of several persons engaged in accounting work also are valuable. You should interview more than one person because the opinion of one may be biased. Talk with former students who accepted positions both in public and private accounting and remained in it, those who voluntarily switched from public accounting to the business field, and experienced accountants who started in the business field and continued in it.

Students having no personal connections through which interviews for this purpose can be arranged will find that a few letters addressed to personnel directors of public accounting firms and corporations explaining why an interview is requested will generally produce favorable responses. Accounting professors and college placement directors have many business connections and are able to direct students to persons who can be of help.

Through these interviews or summer and part-time experience, students can gain a clearer conception of where their interest lies, thus enabling them to select more intelligently the firms and companies they wish to interview on campus.

COLLEGE PLACEMENT DEPARTMENTS

The primary purpose of college placement departments is to assist graduating students in obtaining positions, but their services extend beyond that, and students should not wait until their senior year to find out about them. Placement directors are often able to suggest summer employment possibilities and offer assistance in career decisions, including suggestions concerning subjects that should be taken to meet requirements for positions in which a student expresses interest.

Each year, companies send representatives to college campuses, especially those with the most prestigious accounting departments, to interview seniors seeking employment after graduation. The placement director and the staff of the department are responsible for arranging interviews. Recruiters usually bring with them literature describing their company's policies for hiring, promotion, and other information about the firm, company, or government agency. College placement departments have a supply of these brochures available for students desiring to learn about companies in advance of interviews. Students who read these brochures shortly before being interviewed will be able to ask better questions and obtain more information from interviewers than those who enter an interview "cold." Furthermore, they will be more effective during the interviews and be better able to arrive at sound employment decisions.

Recruiters are chosen at least partially because they can communicate well with today's college students. Because they often are just a few years older than the persons they are interviewing, these recruiters are in an excellent position to give an accurate picture of what the transition from college to employment is like.

College placement directors are sincerely interested in assisting students in securing jobs in which they will be successful, and students should take advantage of the valuable services they offer.

INTERVIEWS

The interview is the focal point of getting a job. It is a meeting of a prospective employer and employee, and contrary to the thinking of many young people, it is not a "one-way street." Interviewers are as anxious to find applicants meeting their employment standards as applicants are to obtain positions offering good experience and advancement possibilities. This mutuality of interests requires complete frankness on the part of both the interviewer and the applicant. Employment arrangements predicated upon false or erroneous representations are generally of short duration.

Naturally, employers want to know all about each applicant before offering him or her a position. They endeavor to determine during the course of an interview the applicant's interest, goals, technical background, college grades, college and community activities, personality, ability to use language grammatically and effectively, ability to get along well with others, willingness and capacity to accept responsibility, and sense of loyalty. Sometimes testing devices are used as an aid in making selections, but more often employment decisions are made solely on the basis of personal reaction and the evaluation of the interviewer.

Similarly, applicants want to know all about each prospective employer before reaching a decision concerning an employment offer. They inquire about the nature of the work, the location where they will be stationed, the extent of traveling involved, whether training programs are provided, whether rapid advancement can be expected, whether the prospective employer follows the practice of making advancements from within the ranks, and if so, whether such advancement is based on merit or length of service. Applicants are justified in asking these and other pertinent questions in order to evaluate and compare both immediate and future possibilities with different employers.

The time allotted for interviewing each student on college campuses is usually thirty minutes. During this relatively short time, the matters mentioned are discussed, and, at least insofar as the employer is concerned, tentative employment decisions are made. However, employers do not customarily make offers to students at the time of the campus interview. Those students considered good prospects are usually invited to visit one of the plants or offices of the employers at the employers' expense. Such visits provide an opportunity for employers to further evaluate the students and for the students to meet people with whom they might be working. After the office visit, the student is informed of the result, and when an offer is made, the student is generally given several weeks to consider it before a reply is required.

Of course not all students or beginners can obtain positions through campus interviews since only larger organizations have college recruitment programs and even those seldom send recruiters to all colleges. For the many students and others who do not obtain positions through campus interviews, office interviews can be arranged by correspondence. June graduates should try to arrange for interviews several months before graduation. They will find that Christmas and spring vacations are excellent times to visit the offices of prospective employers and that definite appointments in advance will prove advantageous. Thirty minutes to two hours or more are generally required for office interviews.

There is no fundamental difference between campus interviews and office interviews, except that final employment decisions are made by employers at office interviews. In each instance, the time element is important. The time allotted for interviews is relatively short for an employer to size up an applicant and for an applicant to learn what an employer has to offer. Yet during this short period, applicants must be able to create a favorable impression. If they are unable to do so, they will have difficulty in obtaining worthwhile positions. Therefore, an applicant would be well advised to find out as much as possible about prospective employers prior to taking interviews. If company literature is available, it should be read. A general knowledge of a prospective employer's personnel practices, methods of operation, products sold or services performed, and the location of plants and offices will provide a background for an applicant to ask intelligent questions during an interview. Knowledge of this kind generates self-confidence and helps to create a favorable impression on interviewers.

An interview is more than a "talk fest." It starts from the moment the interviewer first sees the applicant. Poise, grace, appearance, and assurance can be identified at the time of introduction. The applicant's interest, which is an important factor, is determined by the general attitude evidenced, the questions asked, and the way they are asked. Careless or inappropriate dress, lack of poise and assurance, and inability to speak fluently, grammatically, and effectively are factors most easily ascertained by interviewers.

Applicants should be prepared to answer questions relating to college grades. It is noteworthy that in the field of accounting, employers—particularly those interviewing beginners for staff positions in public accounting—generally place importance on grades as an indicator of potential. Consequently, applicants are frequently asked questions concerning their cumulative average in all subjects and their cumulative average in accounting subjects. Sometimes they are also asked to submit copies of their college records showing the marks received in each subject. Students and graduates can obtain copies of these records from their colleges. Those having good grades should be prepared to submit their college records to prospective employers during interviews, and those who took some or all of the objective tests forming part of the AICPA College Testing Program should also be prepared to furnish the scores they attained on those tests.

While it is true that employers in the accounting field stress the importance of scholastic attainment, college grades are not necessarily the determining factor when making employment decisions. An applicant's personality and characteristics in relation to the position are equally important and often the determining factors.

Employers expect applicants to put their best foot forward. Accordingly, an applicant should not hesitate to explain a below-average scholastic record if there is justifiable reason for it. For example, if the overall average grade stems from poor marks during the first two years followed by a notable improvement during the last two years, this should be pointed out. Similarly, if such grades are attributable to part-time work that interfered with time for study, this might be mentioned. Applicants should also mention scholastic attainments and extracurricular activities when these things will bolster their application. Such explanations, when tactfully made, have the added advantage of indicating ability to deal effectively with others. Obviously, if such explanations are presented the wrong way, they would be better left unsaid.

APPLICATION LETTERS

An application letter serves as a means of presenting the qualifications of an applicant to an employer. Basically, it is not an application for a position but a request for an interview. This is true even though it may have been written in response to an advertisement, because an employment offer is seldom made prior to a personal interview. Whether an interview is granted often depends on the way the request is made. Certainly, it is safe to assume that a courteous letter setting forth briefly and clearly an applicant's qualifications will be more likely to result in a favorable response than a careless letter containing grammatical errors and misspelled words. Many personnel directors can attest to the fact that letters of the latter variety are not uncommon.

Perhaps a few general observations concerning the preparation of application letters may prove helpful. In the first place, application letters should vary in composition and presentation according to the circumstances surrounding each particular case and according to the writing ability and personality of the writer.

Letters imparting a personal touch will create greater interest on the part of the readers than formal ones. This personal approach can be achieved at the outset by addressing letters to an individual by name and by using that person's title, if any. The salutation "Dear Mr. Jones," for example, is more direct and consequently better than "Dear Sir." When writing, be sure that the person's name is spelled correctly. Most people dislike seeing their names misspelled. Likewise, using the first person when writing application letters is customary and warmer than using the third person.

Sometimes application letters are written to employers at the suggestion of employees, former employees, or others. Mentioning the name of the person who offered the suggestion generally has value. However, as a matter of courtesy and prudence, permission should be obtained before using names in this way or even as personal references in application letters.

Typewritten application letters are preferable to ones written in longhand, but the latter are acceptable if written legibly. If typewritten, the letter should be signed with pen and ink.

PERSONAL RESUMES

Applicants should submit certain basic facts about themselves to employers. These include name and address, age, educational background, experience, and data available for employment. This basic information should be summarized in the form of a personal resume.

Many applicants have their resumes printed commercially or otherwise duplicated, then attach copies of letters of application. When resumes are included, the application letters themselves can be shorter and the contents slanted toward the particular opening for which application is being made. Most employers prefer short application letters with resumes attached to long letters detailing background information. However, sending a resume without a cover letter or using a preprinted application letter is considered poor practice.

Care should be taken in preparing resumes. The appearance and the information supplied can create either a favorable or unfavorable impression.

THE FIRST FEW MONTHS

Getting started in a new job can be, and usually is, an interesting experience, but for beginners with little or no business experience, it may not be exactly easy. Difficulties encountered in getting started seldom stem from a lack of interest on the part of employers or uncooperativeness on the part of fellow employees but rather from the natural tensions that grow out of learning many new things in different surroundings and making new associations within a short time.

A beginner may have the benefit of a formal orientation training program that gives insight into the departmental organization of the employer and offers the new accountant an opportunity to meet a number of key personnel with whom he or she will later have dealings. But with or without such a program, trainees will have no difficulty during the initial employment period if they approach their jobs with earnestness, interest, and a willingness to learn.

Normally, the transition from school to the business world is uneventful and follows pretty much the pattern the beginner might anticipate from preemployment discussions with the employer. Sometimes, though, at the outset, things may not work out as expected. Beginners may first be assigned to inconsequential or routine work, possibly quite alien to the positions for which they were employed. As a result, they may feel frustrated and discontented, especially if the importance of the new job was given a buildup at the time of hire. However, such assignments may be of short duration to fill in while arrangements are being completed for the beginners to take up the responsibilities for which they were employed. Although considerate employers should explain this in advance, a wise beginner will accept such an assignment in good grace for a short time before seeking an explanation. The answer probably will become apparent without inquiry, and, in the meantime, nothing has been lost since any experience beginners receive will add to their general knowledge of business. If the answer is not forthcoming within a reasonable time, the beginner in all fairness should discuss this matter with the employer before seeking another position.

Obviously, new jobs require certain adjustments. For beginners who have had no previous full-time employment, the usual 9 A.M. to 5 P.M. office hours may seem somewhat long and confining, especially during the first few days when they have no fixed duties or responsibilities. This generally changes when their jobs take on meaning and they become better acquainted with other employees. Also during the first few days, beginners hesitate to ask questions, being unsure whether their questions concern things they are expected to know about and whether their questioning will indicate ignorance. Beginners might be compared with people who are given a jigsaw puzzle of a ship to assemble without being told whether the ship is a sailing vessel, motor launch, or destroyer or whether it is of ancient or modern vintage. In these circumstances, matching the first few pieces causes difficulty, but as more pieces are assembled, the job gradually becomes easier and more interesting.

During the early stages of employment, beginners are observed critically. The manner in which they approach their work and deal with other employees is quickly noted. An attitude that can be described as ''I've done my part by reporting for work; now its's up to you to teach me'' is the best possible way to alienate employers and co-workers. On the other hand, those entering their duties with interest and enthusiasm will find that they are given credit for doing well and are excused for their weaknesses. But, of course, this does not go on forever; soon they are expected to do things right and take full responsibility for errors. They are instinctively catalogued by employers as good, average, or poor, and once so classified it becomes increasingly difficult to change first impressions.

CHAPTER 11

PROFESSIONAL ORGANIZATIONS

Older professions have been represented by societies and guilds for centuries. Newer ones, as they developed, likewise found need for unified action and formed professional associations. The objectives of most professional associations may be summed up as follows: to set adequate admission requirements, to maintain high standards of performance, to formulate and enforce codes of ethics and conduct, to provide a means for pooling professional knowledge, to foster good public relations, and to engender a spirit of professional understanding and cooperation among members practicing their professions.

You should note that differences of opinion exist concerning who should be classified as members of the accounting profession. Some consider that only those practicing public accounting should be so classified. Others would place only certified public accountants and their equivalents in other countries in that category and then classify them as professional accountants, irrespective of whether they are engaged in public, private, or government accounting. However, in common usage, the term *accounting professional* encompasses all accountants performing work or offering services requiring more than a limited knowledge of accounting theory and practice, and this broad definition has been followed in describing professional accounting organizations in this chapter.

ACCOUNTANTS FOR THE PUBLIC INTEREST (API)

1625 I Street, NW, Suite 717
Washington, DC 20006
Phone: 202-659-3797

Accountants for the Public Interest was founded in 1975 to encourage public interest in accounting activities in the United States. The API endeavors to convince leaders in the accounting profession to encourage and support the activities of public interest accounting groups. The twelve hundred member association also initiates studies on national issues and coordinates the efforts of local organizations involved in such cases.

AMERICAN ACCOUNTING ASSOCIATION (AAA)

5717 Bessie Drive
Sarasota, FL 34233
Phone: 813-921-7747

The AAA, which was founded in 1916, is primarily an association for college accounting teachers, although its membership, which numbers approximately fifteen thousand, not only includes teachers of accounting but many public and industrial accountants. Students may become associate members; this membership entitles them to receive the association's quarterly publication, the *Accounting Review*, and to attend the annual meeting without voting privileges. One of the primary objectives of the AAA is to promote research and education in accounting. In order to carry out this objective, the AAA sponsors a fellowship program for Ph.D. candidates in accounting.

AMERICAN INSTITUTE OF CERTIFIED PUBLIC ACCOUNTANTS (AICPA)

1211 Avenue of the Americas
New York, NY 10036
Phone: 212-575-6200

The AICPA is the oldest and largest professional association of public accountants in the United States, with over 280,000 members. The AICPA was founded in 1887 as the American Association of Public Accountants, nine years before the first CPA law was enacted in the United States. Its history has paralleled the growth and recognition of the profession in the United States, and it has contributed substantially to the profession's rapid expansion and sound development. The broad scope of the institute's objectives is carried out by about a hundred committees. The committees deal with accounting standards, auditing standards, federal taxation, management advisory services, professional ethics, and computer services, to name just a few.

The AICPA publishes *The Journal of Accountancy* as well as several bulletins to keep its membership informed about professional matters and membership activities. The institute also publishes numerous books, pamphlets, and pronouncements on subjects of professional significance.

This organization plays a vital part in accounting education and in preparing CPA examinations. Its accounting and auditing committees conduct research and issue standards and guidelines relative to the treatment of new accounting and auditing requirements. These standards are considered authoritative and are followed by professional accountants.

The institute maintains a library of over one hundred thousand books and pamphlets on accounting and related subjects. It offers a broad range of services to its membership. Its Code of Professional Ethics, to which all members must subscribe, is rigidly enforced.

Unquestionably, the American Institute of Certified Public Accountants ranks high among professional accounting organizations. It provides a necessary meeting ground for all certified public accountants and fosters the growth and prestige of the profession through the encouragement of high professional standards.

AMERICAN SOCIETY OF WOMEN ACCOUNTANTS (ASWA)

35 E. Wacker Drive, Suite 2250
Chicago, IL 60601
Phone: 312-726-9030

This professional society of women accountants, educators, and others engaged in accounting work was founded in 1938. The ASWA currently has more than seventy-three hundred members. Its publications are the *Coordinator*, a monthly bulletin, and *The Woman CPA*, a quarterly journal.

AMERICAN WOMAN'S SOCIETY OF CERTIFIED PUBLIC ACCOUNTANTS (AWSCPA)

111 E. Wacker Drive, Suite 600
Chicago, IL 60601
Phone: 312-644-6610

This organization was founded in 1933 and has a membership of over five thousand. The society has three forms of membership. Women who hold CPA certificates and are citizens of the United States are full members. Those women who have passed the CPA exam but do not have certificates may be associate members; and women holding degrees comparable to CPA certificates but who are not United States citizens are entitled to be international associates. AWSCPA works to improve women's competence in the accounting profession and to make the business community aware of the professional capabilities of the woman CPA. The society also maintains a register of all women CPAs and conducts occasional statistical surveys of its members. Its publications are the *AWSCPA Newsletter* and *The Woman CPA*.

ASSOCIATION OF GOVERNMENT ACCOUNTANTS (AGA)

601 Wythe Street, #204
Alexandria, VA 22314
Phone: 703-684-6931

The Association of Government Accountants (AGA) is a professional society of accountants, auditors, controllers, and budget officers employed by federal, state, and local governments. The AGA was founded in 1950 and has about thirteen thousand members. The association sponsors competitions, bestows awards, engages in research, and offers a placement service. Its publications are *Government Financial Management Topics* and *The Government Accountants Journal*.

FINANCIAL ACCOUNTING FOUNDATION (FAF)

(Umbrella group for Financial Accounting Standards Board)
401 Merritt, #7
Norwalk, CT 06586
Phone: 203-847-0700

The Financial Accounting Standards Board (FASB) was established in 1972 by the AICPA as the body responsible for formulating accounting standards that would be enforceable by the AICPA rules of conduct of the Code of Professional Ethics. It operates under a tripartite structure for establishing financial accounting standards in the private sector.

The Board of Trustees of the Financial Accounting Foundation and its various committees appoint the members of the Standards Board and Advisory Council, raise funds, scrutinize budgets, and exercise general oversight, except with regard to technical decisions of the FASB, for which the Standards Board is solely responsible under the foundation bylaws.

The Standards Board is independent of government and all other business and professional organizations. Members of the board serve full time and are required to sever all previous business or professional connections.

By means of its pronouncements—statements, interpretations, discussion memoranda, exposure drafts, technical bulletins, and research reports—the FASB is able to carry out its mission; that is, to establish a body of underlying theory for financial accounting and reporting.

FINANCIAL EXECUTIVES INSTITUTE (FEI)

P.O. Box 1938
Ten Madison Avenue
Morristown, NJ 07960
Phone: 201-898-4600

The Financial Executives Institute is an organization consisting primarily of controllers, treasurers, and other financial officers in diversified business and industry in the United States, Canada, and Puerto Rico. Organized in 1931 as the Controllers Institute of America, it now has 92 chapters and a membership of almost 13,320.

The purposes of the institute are to develop a progressive concept of financial management that is adequate to meet the requirements of modern business; to provide financial executives with a forum through which they may exchange ideas in the field of business management; to constitute an articulate body of management on matters within the scope of the financial executive's responsibility; and, in so doing, to contribute toward soundness in business, education, government, and the economy.

FEI publishes a bimonthly magazine, the *Financial Executive*, and through its research arm, the Financial Executives Research Foundation, it conducts fundamental research and publishes authoritative material in the field of business management.

INSTITUTE OF INTERNAL AUDITORS (IIA)

249 Maitland Avenue
Altamonte Springs, FL 32701
Phone: 407-830-7600

The Institute of Internal Auditors is an organization of persons in internal auditing positions. The IIA was founded in 1941 and has over thirty-two thousand members.

The broad scope of IIA activities is indicated by the large number of committees that help carry out the objectives of the institute. It also sponsors educational seminars and conferences for all levels of internal audit staff and management as well as for general management. IIA publishes *The Internal Auditor*, *IIA Today*, and various research reports and textbooks.

NATIONAL ASSOCIATION OF ACCOUNTANTS (NAA)

Ten Paragon Drive
Montvale, NJ 07645
Phone: 201-573-9000

This organization was founded in 1919 as the National Association of Cost Accountants. Its name was changed to the National Association of Accountants in 1957 in order to more accurately describe its activities, which for some years have been the study of problems of industrial accounting including, but not limited to, cost accounting. Essentially, this association is a cooperative movement for the development of sound industrial management accounting and for the mutual self-betterment of its members.

The NAA has about 85,000 members and 328 chapters, including a few in foreign countries. Most of its members are management accountants working for business organizations, but a number of public accountants, government accountants, and accounting teachers are also members.

Membership services are provided both by the chapters and the national organization. A research department is maintained at national headquarters, and the research staff prepares reports covering all fields of management accounting.

The association also conducts a substantial continuing education program and provides a technical service and a question and answer service for its members. Its official monthly publication, *Management Accounting*, covers a broad range of subjects relating to financial management.

NATIONAL ASSOCIATION OF BLACK ACCOUNTANTS (NABA)

300 I Street, NE, Suite 107
Washington, DC 20002
Phone: 202-682-0222

The NABA is an association of three thousand CPAs, accountants, and students of accounting concerned with enhancing opportunities for minorities in the accounting profession. Its programs include free income tax assistance for low-income wage earners; consulting to minority businesses; and technical seminars and lectures. The NABA publishes *News Plus*, a bimonthly newsletter.

NATIONAL ASSOCIATION OF STATE BOARDS OF ACCOUNTANCY (NASBA)

545 Fifth Avenue
New York, NY 10017
Phone: 212-490-3868

The National Association of State Boards of Accountancy, founded in 1908, is one of the oldest professional accounting associations in the United States. It serves as a forum for communication among state boards of accountancy and is an organization through which state and territorial boards assist their members in the practice of accountancy. Tha NASBA helps its member state boards obtain services needed for the administration of public accountancy laws and the protection of the public interest.

NATIONAL SOCIETY OF PUBLIC ACCOUNTANTS (NSPA)

1010 N. Fairfax Street
Alexandria, VA 22314
Phone: 703-549-6400

The NSPA is a professional society of public accountants. Its membership is about 23,000, and it has fifty-two chapters. The NSPA promotes high educational standards for its members. It conducts correspondence courses and awards thirty-three scholarships annually to accounting students. The society publishes *National Public Accountant; Washington Reporter;* and *Income and Fees of Accountants in Public*

Practice (triennial). It has also published a portfolio of accounting systems for small and medium-sized businesses.

STATE CPA SOCIETIES

State societies of certified public accountants were organized shortly after the various states enacted legislation that provided for the issuance of CPA certificates. The first society was formed in New York State in 1897, and by 1929, each state had its own society. There are many CPAs who belong to both their own state society and the American Institute of Certified Public Accountants.

The objectives of state societies are, in general, the same as those of the institute, and their activities within their states generally parallel and supplement those carried on by the institute on a national level. Because CPA laws and regulations come under jurisdiction of individual states, the work of state societies in maintaining high educational, ethical, and professional standards is vital.

Programs of state societies differ, but basically they are all geared to give practical assistance to members in day-to-day work. Most conduct professional development programs for members. Research is carried on by their technical committees, and the results are considered at general or technical meetings or are made available to the membership through published articles.

RECOMMENDED READING

Adams, Bettie M. "Accounting Systems: An Emerging Career Path." In *Collected Papers of the Annual Meeting, April 21–23, 1988, Knoxville, Tennessee.* American Accounting Association, Southeast Region, 1988.

Accounting: A Career for Women. Chicago: American Woman's Society of Certified Public Accountants.

Accounting and Finance Salary Survey and Career Planning Guide. Source Finance, 1988.

"AICPA Industry Members Surveyed," *Journal of Accountancy* 165 (June 1988): 22.

Ambrosio, Johanna. "Hot Companies to Work For." *New Accountant* 4, (December 1988): 4, 6–8.

Brennan, Patrick J. "Welcome to the Real World: Making the Transition from Public to Private Accounting." *Pennsylvania CPA Journal* 58 (Spring 1988): 12–14.

Broden, Barry C., and Robert M. Rosen. "Tax Career Path after TRA '86." *New Accountant* 4 (October 1988): 18, 20–21, 23.

Brunning, Sally. "Babies Can Still Be Bad for the Woman Accountant's Career." *Accountant* 5812 (April 1988): 12–13.

Collins, Stephen H. "Blacks in the Profession." *Journal of Accountancy* 165 (February 1988): 38, 40–44.

Connaghan, C.J. "Achieving Success." *CGA Magazine* 22 (July 1988): 24–26.

Cuppett, William T. "Consulting Opportunities in the Health Care Industry." *Management Advisor* 1 (Spring 1988): 20–25.

"Demand for Accounting Graduates Keeps Pace with Supply." *Journal of Accountancy* 166 (October 1988): 96.

Dillon, Ray D., and Paul E. White. "Model for Job Selection." *New Accountant* 3 (March 1988): 44–47.

Douma, Irene K. "Is the Certified Public Accountant a Professional? The Perceptions of CPAs, Financial Executives, Bankers, Financial Analysts and Attorneys." Ph.D. diss., City University of New York, 1982.

Emerson, James C. *Careers in Public Accounting: A Comprehensive Comparison of the Big Eight Review.*

Finerman, Scott C., and Roland L. Madison. "Beyond the Hype." *New Accountant* 4 (November 1988): 34–36.

Haswell, Stephen and Scott Holmes. "Accounting Graduate Employment Choice." *Chartered Accountant in Australia* 59 (August 1988): 63–67.

Horizons for the Tax Professional. New York: Price Waterhouse, 1985.

Imhoff, Eugene A. "Planning Academic Accounting Careers." *Issues in Accounting Education* 3 (Fall 1988): 286–301.

Joseph, Cynthia J. "Considering State Auditing." *New Accountant* 3 (February 1988): 33–34, 36.

Levy, Elliott S. "Educators and Practitioners: A Faculty Internship Experience." *Massachusetts CPA Review* 62 (Fall 1988): 11, 32–36.

Liebtag, Bill. "CPAs in Government." *Journal of Accountancy* 165 (January 1988): 55–57.

MacIver, Brian H. "How to Start a Professional in Residence Program." *Massachusetts CPA Review* 62 (Fall 1988): 11, 30–31.

"Managing Your Career." *CMA* 62 (November 1988): 16–19.

Marquette, R. Penny, and Alvin Lieberman. "Future Women Accountants: The Best and the Brightest—or the Most Naive?" *Woman CPA* 50 (October 1988): 12–15.

Mautz, R.K. "Some Thoughts on Balance." *Accounting Horizons* 2 (December 1988): 136–39.

McInnes, Mary, and Beatrice Sanders. *Supply of Accounting Graduates and the Demand for Public Accounting Recruits, 1988.* New York: American Institute of Certified Public Accountants, 1988.

McKee, Thomas E., and W. Edward Stead. "Managing the Professional Accountant." *Journal of Accountancy* 166 (July 1988): 76–78, 80ff.

Previts, Gary John. *Quiet Revolution: Accounting in the Next Decade.* Mary Ball Washington Forum Series in Accounting Education, vol. 1, 1983–1984. Pensacola, Fla.: 1985.

Rosen, Herbert H. "Accountants in the DEA." *New Accountant* 3 (February 1988): 4–7.

Schmidt, L. Lee. "Economics of Mandatory Five-Year Accounting Education Programs." *Spectrum* (Spring 1988): 11–13.

Solis, William M., and Francine DelVecchio. "Assisting Congress." *New Accountant* 3 (February 1988): 14, 16–18.

Spiotta-DiMare, Loren. "Taking the Green Eyeshades off CPAs." *Executive Business Magazine* (June 1988).

Take the CPA Challenge: Careers in Accounting. New York: American Institute of Certified Public Accountants, Relations with Educators Division, 1988.

von Alten, Judith Walthers. "Diverse Business and Industry Members Find Common Ground." *Outlook* 56 (Spring 1988): 8–13.

Wiegand, Richard. "Perks for the High Achiever." *New Accountant* 4 (December 1988): 10–12.

Woelfel, Charles. "Minority Students: Career Planning and Expectations." *Spectrum* (Fall 1988): 53–55.

Yockey, Dennis W. "So You Want to Be a Forensic Accountant?" *Management Accounting* 70 (November 1988): 19, 22, 25.

SCHOOLS OF BUSINESS ADMINISTRATION WITH DEGREE PROGRAMS IN ACCOUNTING

Students planning careers in accounting should select schools that are appropriately accredited. The National Commission of Accrediting recognizes six regional accrediting associations (the Northeastern, Southern, Middle States, North Central, Northwest, and Western associations) and in the area of business administration (which includes accounting), the American Assembly of Collegiate Schools of Business (AACSB).

State boards of accountancy may allow candidates to take the CPA examination even though they are not graduates of schools accredited by the AACSB or by one of the regional associations recognized by the National Commission on Accrediting. Anyone planning eventually to take the Uniform CPA Examination should have assurance before enrolling in an educational institution that the program selected satisfies the educational requirements for the CPA certificate in the state where the examination will be taken. (A list of the addresses of state boards of accountancy is given in appendix C.)

A list of schools offering courses of study leading to undergraduate or graduate degrees in accounting follows. Because accreditations are continually being earned or changed, you should write to the school about accreditation at the time of your choice. The last line of each listing indicates the level of accreditation that the school has achieved (B = baccalaureate; M = master's).

In April 1982, The American Assembly of Collegiate Schools of Business accredited, for the first time, accounting programs at eighteen colleges. Final approval of the accounting programs occurred at the AACSB annual meeting in April and marked the first time the assembly had accredited any program other than those offering degrees in business administration only.

The AACSB, which has been accrediting business programs since 1916, has accredited three types of accounting programs: type A—bachelor's degree with a concentration in accounting; type B—master's degree in business administration with a concentration in accounting; and type C—master of accounting degree, which includes 150-semester-hour integrated programs.

The AACSB standards for accreditation include requirements that specified portions of the school faculty be qualified as to professional certification and experience as well as academic credentials.

The accreditation program is a joint effort of the AACSB and the accounting profession in that the Accounting Accreditation Committee (AAC) of the AACSB includes representation from the American Institute of CPAs, the American Accounting Association, the National Association of Accountants, and the Financial Executives Institute. A listing of the schools accredited and the types of accounting programs approved (A, B, or C) follows the complete list of schools.

Because they do not grant degrees, two-year community colleges are not included on the list, although they play an increasingly important role in the education of accountants. Many thousands of young people are introduced to accounting in courses at two-year colleges, then complete their accounting education at four-year colleges and graduate schools. To learn whether credits earned at a community college are transferable, ask the college's administrators or check with the four-year school to which you plan to transfer for the remainder of your education. Your state board of accountancy usually can also help you assess the standing of your community college's accounting department.

ACCREDITED SCHOOLS OF THE AMERICAN ASSEMBLY OF COLLEGIATE SCHOOLS OF BUSINESS

The following represents the members of the Accreditation Council of the American Assembly of Collegiate Schools of Business. The last line of each listing indicates the level of accreditation the school has achieved (B = baccalaureate; M = masters).

University of Akron
    College of Business Administration
    Akron, Ohio 44325
    216-375-7442
    BM

University of Alabama
    College of Commerce and
        Business Adminstration
    Manderson Graduate School of
        Business, Box J
    Tuscaloosa, Alabama 35487-9725
    205-348-7443
    BM

University of Alabama at Birmingham
    School of Business
    Graduate School of Management
    UAB Station
    Birmingham, Alabama 35294
    205-934-8810
    BM

University of Alaska–Fairbanks
    School of Management
    Fairbanks, Alaska 99775
    907-474-7461
    BM

University of Alberta
    Faculty of Business
    Faculty of Business Building
    Edmonton, Alberta T6G 2R6
    Canada
    403-432-3901
    BM

Alfred University
    College of Business and
        Administration
    P.O. Box 515
    Alfred, New York 14802
    607-871-2124
    B

Appalachian State University
    John A. Walker College of Business
    Boone, North Carolina 28608
    704-262-2057
    BM

University of Arizona
    College of Business and Public
        Administration
    Tucson, Arizona 85721
    602-621-2165
    BM

Arizona State University
    College of Business
    Tempe, Arizona 85287
    602-965-5516
    BM

University of Arkansas
    College of Business Administration
    Fayetteville, Arkansas 72701
    501-575-4551
    BM

University of Arkansas at Little Rock
    College of Business Administration
    2801 South University Avenue
    Little Rock, Arkansas 72204
    501-569-3357
    BM

Arkansas State University
  College of Business
  P.O. Box 970
  State University, Arkansas 72467
  501-972-3035
Atlanta University
  Graduate School of Business
    Administration
  Atlanta, Georgia 30314
  404-653-8415
  M
Auburn University
  College of Business
  Auburn University, Alabama
    36849-3501
  205-826-4030
  BM
Auburn University at Montgomery
  School of Business
  Montgomery, Alabama 36193
  205-271-9478
  BM
Babson College
  School of Management
  Babson Park, Massachusetts 02157
  617-239-4316
  BM
Ball State University
  College of Business
  Muncie, Indiana 47306
  317-285-8192
  BM
University of Baltimore
  Robert G. Merrick School of
    Business
  140 North Charles Street
  Baltimore, Maryland 21201
  301-625-3255
  BM

Baruch College of the City University
  of New York
  School of Business and Public
    Administration
  17 Lexington Avenue
  New York, New York 10010
  212-725-3116
  BM
Baylor University
  Hankamer School of Business
  Waco, Texas 76798
  817-755-1211
  BM
Bentley College
  Beaver and Forest Streets
  Waltham, Massachusetts 02254
  617-891-2105
  BM
Boise State University
  College of Business
  1910 University Drive
  Boise, Idaho 83725
  208-385-1125
  BM
Boston College
  School of Management
  Chestnut Hill, Massachusetts
    02167
  617-552-8420
  BM
Boston University
  School Management
  685 Commonwealth Avenue
  Boston, Massachusetts 02215
  617-353-2668
  BM
Bowling Green State University
  College of Business Administration
  Bowling Green, Ohio 43403
  419-372-2747
  BM

Bradley University
  College of Business Administration
  Peoria, Illinois 61625
  309-677-2255
  BM

University of Bridgeport
  College of Business and Public
    Management
  Bridgeport, Connecticut 06601
  203-576-4384
  BM

Brigham Young University
  School of Management
  Provo, Utah 84602
  801-378-4122
  BM

The University of Calgary
  Faculty of Management
  2500 University Drive, N.W.
  Calgary, Alberta, Canada T2N 1N4
  403-220-5689
  BM

University of California at Berkeley
  Schools of Business Administration
  Berkeley, California 94720
  415-642-1425
  BM

University of California, Irvine
  Graduate School of Management
  Irvine, California 92717
  714-856-6855
  M

University of California, Los Angeles
  Graduate School of Management
  Los Angeles, California 90024
  213-825-7982
  M

California Polytechnic State
  University, San Luis Obispo
  School of Business
  San Luis Obispo, California 93407
  805-546-2704
  BM

California State University,
  Bakersfield
  School of Business and Public
    Administration
  9001 Stockdale Highway
  Bakersfield, California 93309-1099
  805-833-2157
  BM

California State University, Chico
  School of Business
  Chico, California 95929-0001
  916-895-6271
  BM

California State University, Fresno
  School of Business and
    Administrative Sciences
  Fresno, California 93740-0008
  290-294-2482
  BM

California State University, Fullerton
  School of Business Administration
    and Economics
  Fullerton, California 92634
  714-773-2592
  BM

Calilfornia State University, Hayward
  School of Business and Economics
  Hayward, California 94542
  415-881-3291
  BM

California State University, Long
  Beach
  School of Business Administration
  Long Beach, California 90840
  213-985-5306
  BM

California State University, Los
Angeles
School of Business and Economics
5151 State University Drive
Room F124, Simpson Tower
Los Angeles, California 90032
213-343-2800
BM

California State University, Northridge
School of Business Administration
and Economics
Northridge, Caifornia 91330
818-885-2455
BM

California State University,
Sacramento
School of Business and Public
Administration
6000 J Street
Sacramento, California 95819
916-278-6578
BM

Canisius College
School of Business Administration
Buffalo, New York 14208
716-888-2164
BM

Carnegie Mellon University
Graduate School of Industrial
Administration
Pittsburgh, Pennsylvania 15213
412-268-2265
BM

Case Western Reserve University
Weatherhead School of
Management
Cleveland, Ohio 44106
216-368-2046
BM

University of Central Arkansas
College of Business Administration
Conway, Arkansas 72032
501-450-3106
B

University of Central Florida
College of Business Administration
P.O. Box 25000
Orlando, Florida 32816
407-275-2181
BM

Central Michigan University
School of Business Administration
Mt. Pleasant, Michigan 48859
517-774-3337
BM

University of Chicago
Graduate School of Business
1101 East 58th Street
Chicago, Illinois 60637
312-702-7121
M

University of Cincinna.i
College of Business Administration
Cincinnati, Ohio 45221-0020
513-556-7001
BM

Clark University
Graduate School of Management
Worcester, Massachusetts 01610
617-793-7670
BM

Clarkson University
School of Management
Potsdam, New York 13676
315-268-2300
BM

Clemson University
  College of Commerce and Industry
  Clemson, South Carolina
    29634-1301
    803-656-3178
    BM
Cleveland State University
  James J. Nance College of
    Business Administration
  Cleveland, Ohio 44115
    216-687-3786
    BM
College of Charleston
  School of Business and Economics
  9 Liberty Street
  Charleston, South Carolina 29424
    803-792-5627
    B
College of William and Mary
  School of Business Administration
  Williamsburg, Virginia 23185
    804-253-4001
    BM
University of Colorado, Boulder
  College of Business and
    Administration and
  Graduate School of Business
    Administration
  Campus Box 419
  Boulder, Colorado 80309-0419
    303-492-1807
    BM
University of Colorado at Denver
  College of Business and
    Administration and
  Graduate School of Business
    Administration
  1200 Larimer St., Campus Box 165
  Denver, Colorado 80204-5300
    303-628-1205
    BM

Colorado State University
  College of Business
  Fort Collins, Colorado 80523
    303-491-6471
    BM
Columbia University
  Graduate School of Business
  101 Uris Hall
  New York, New York 10027
    212-854-3401
    M
University of Connecticut
  School of Business Administration
    U-41D
  Storrs, Connecticut 06268
    203-486-2317
    BM
Cornell University
  Johnson Graduate School of
    Management
  303 Malott Hall
  Ithaca, New York 14853
    607-255-6418
    M
Creighton University
  College of Business Administration
  Omaha, Nebraska 68178
    402-280-2852
    BM
Dartmouth College
  The Amos Tuck School of
    Business Administration
  Hanover, New Hampshire 03755
    603-646-2460
    M
University of Dayton
  School of Business Administration
  Dayton, Ohio 45469
    513-229-3731
    BM

University of Delaware
  College of Business and Economics
  Newark, Delaware 19716
  302-451-2551
  BM

University of Denver
  College of Business Administration
  Graduate School of Business and
    Public Management
  Denver, Colorado 80208
  303-871-3411
  BM

DePaul University
  College of Commerce
  25 East Jackson Boulevard
  Chicago, Illinois 60604
  312-341-6783
  BM

University of Detroit
  College of Business and
    Administration
  4001 W. McNichols Road
  Detroit, Michigan 48221
  313-927-1200
  BM

Drake University
  College of Business and Public
    Administration
  Aliber Hall
  Des Moines, Iowa 50311
  515-271-2871
  BM

Drexel University
  College of Business and
    Administration
  Philadelphia, Pennsylvania 19104
  215-895-2110
  BM

Duke University
  Fuqua School of Business
  Durham, North Carolina 27706
  919-684-2495
  M

Duquesne University
  School of Business and
    Administration
  Pittsburgh, Pennsylvania 15282
  412-434-5157
  BM

East Carolina University
  School of Business
  Greenville, North Carolina
    27858-4353
  919-757-6966
  BM

East Tennessee State University
  College of Business
  Box 23470A
  Johnson City, Tennessee 37614
  615-929-5489
  BM

East Texas State University
  College of Business and
    Technology
  Commerce, Texas 75428
  214-886-5189
  BM

Eastern Michigan University
  College of Business
  Ypsilanti, Michigan 48197
  313-487-4140
  BM

Eastern Washington University
  School of Business
  Cheney, Washington 99004
  509-359-2455
  BM

Emory University
  School of Business Administration
  Atlanta, Georgia 30322
  404-727-6377
  BM

University of Florida
  College of Business Administration
  Matherly Hall, Room 224
  Gainesville, Florida 32611
  904-392-2397
  BM

Florida Atlantic University
  College of Business and Public
    Administration
  Boca Raton, Florida 33431
  407-367-3630
  BM

Florida International University
  College of Business Administration
  Miami, Florida 33199
  305-554-2754
  BM

Florida State University
  College of Business
  Tallahassee, Florida 32306-1042
  904-644-3090
  BM

Fordham University
  Graduate School of Business
    Administration, Room 624
  113 West 60th Street
  New York, New York 10023
  212-841-5521
  BM

Fort Lewis College
  School of Business Administration
  Durango, Colorado 81301
  303-247-7294
  B

George Mason University
  School of Business Administration
  4400 University Drive
  Farifax, Virgina 22030
  703-323-2760
  BM

George Washington University
  School of Government and
    Business Administration
  Washington, D.C. 20052
  202-994-6380
  BM

Georgetown University
  School of Business Administration
  207 Old North
  Washington, D.C. 20057
  202-687-3509
  BM

University of Georgia
  College of Business Administration
  Athens, Georgia 30602
  404-542-8100
  BM

Georgia Institute of Technology
  College of Management
  225 North Avenue, N.W.
  Atlanta, Georgia 30332-0520
  404-894-2601
  BM

Georgia Southern College
  School of Business
  Statesboro, Georgia 30460
  912-618-5106
  BM

Georgia State University
  College of Business Administration
  University Plaza
  Atlanta, Georgia 30303
  404-651-26002
  BM

Harvard University
  Graduate School of Business
    Administration
  Soldiers Field
  Boston, Massachusetts 02163
  617-495-6550
  M

University of Hawaii
  College of Business Administration
  2404 Maile Way
  Honolulu, Hawaii 96822
  808-948-8377
  BM

Hofstra University
  School of Business
  1000 Fulton Avenue
  Hampstead, New York 11550
  516-560-5015
  BM

University of Houston at Clear Lake
  School of Business and Public
    Administration
  2700 Bay Area Boulevard
  Houston, Texas 77058
  713-488-9330
  BM

University of Houston–University Park
  College of Business Administration
  #350 Melcher Hall
  4800 Calhoun Street
  Houston, Texas 77204
  713-749-3297
  BM

Howard University
  School of Business and Public
    Administration
  Washington, D.C. 20059
  202-636-5105
  BM

Idaho State University
  College of Business
  Pocatello, Idaho 83209
  208-236-3585
  BM

University of Illinois at Chicago
  College of Business Administration
  Box 4348 (M/C075)
  Chicago, Illinois 60680
  312-996-2671
  BM

University of Illinois at
    Urbana-Champaign
  College of Commerce and
    Business Administration
  260 Commerce West
  1206 S. Sixth Street
  Champaign, Illinois 61820
  217-333-2747
  BM

Illinois State University
  College of Business
  Normal, Illinois 61761
  309-438-2251
  BM

Indiana State University
  School of Business
  Terre Haute, Indiana 47809
  812-237-2000
  BM

Indiana University
  The School of Business
  The Graduate School of Business
  Bloomington, Indiana 47405
  812-335-8489
  BM

Indiana University–Northwest
Division of Business and
Economics
3400 Broadway
Gary, Indiana 46408
219-980-6633
BM

Indiana University–Purdue University
at Fort Wayne
Division of Business and
Economics
2101 Coliseum Boulevard East
Fort Wayne, Indiana 46805
219-481-6461
BM

Indiana University at South Bend
Division of Business and
Economics
P.O. Box 7111
South Bend, Indiana 46634
219-237-4217
BM

University of Iowa
College of Business Administration
111 Phillips Hall
Iowa City, Iowa 52242
319-335-0866
BM

James Madison University
College of Business
Harrisonburg, Virginia 22807
703-568-6341
BM

John Carroll University
School of Business
Cleveland, Ohio 44118
216-397-4391
BM

University of Kansas
School of Business
Lawrence, Kansas 66045
913-864-3795
BM

Kansas State University
College of Business Administration
Manhattan, Kansas 66506
913-532-7190
BM

Kent State University
College of Business Administration
Graduate School of Management
Kent, Ohio 44242
216-672-2772
BM

University of Kentucky
College of Business and Economics
Lexington, Kentucky 40506-0034
606-257-8939
BM

Lamar University
College of Business
P.O. Box 10059
Beaumont, Texas 77710
409-880-8603
BM

Lehigh University
College of Business and Economics
Bethlehem, Pennsylvania 18015
215-758-3402
BM

Louisiana State University
College of Business Administration
Baton Rouge, Louisiana 70803
504-388-5297
BM

Louisiana Tech University
  College of Administration and
    Business
  Box 10318
  Ruston, Louisiana 71272
  318-257-4526
  BM

University of Louisville
  School of Business
  Louisville, Kentucky 40292
  502-588-6443
  BM

University of Lowell
  College of Management Science
  Lowell, Massachusetts 01854
  508-452-5000 X2979
  BM

Loyola College in Maryland
  Joseph A. Sellinger School of
    Business and Management
  4501 North Charles Street
  Baltimore, Maryland 21210
  301-323-1010 X2301
  BM

Loyola Marymount University
  College of Business Administration
  Los Angeles, California 90045
  213-642-2731
  BM

Loyola University
  School of Business Administration
  Water Tower Campus
  820 North Michigan Avenue
  Chicago, Illinois 60611
  312-670-3130
  BM

Loyola University
  Joseph A. Butt, S.J. College of
    Business Administration
  New Orleans, Louisiana 70118
  504-865-3547
  BM

University of Maine
  College of Business Administration
  Orono, Maine 04469-0158
  207-581-1968
  BM

Marquette University
  College of Business Administration
  Milwaukee, Wisconsin 53233
  414-224-7141
  BM

University of Maryland
  College of Business and
    Management
  College Park, Maryland 20742
  301-454-5383
  BM

University of Massachusetts–Amherst
  School of Management
  Amherst, Massachusetts 01003
  413-549-4930
  BM

Massachusetts Institute of Technology
  Alfred P. Sloan School of
    Management
  Cambridge, Massachusetts 02139
  617-253-2932
  BM

McNeese State University
  College of Business
  P.O. Box 92140
  Lake Charles, Louisiana 70609
  318-475-5514
  BM

Memphis State University
  The Fogelman College of Business
    and Economics
  Memphis, Tennessee 38152
  901-678-2431
  BM

University of Miami
School of Business Administration
P.O. Box 248027
Coral Gables, Florida 33124
305-284-4643
BM

Miami University
School of Business Administration
Oxford, Ohio 45056
513-529-3631
BM

University of Michigan
School of Business Administration
Graduate School of Business
Administration
Ann Arbor, Michigan 48109-1234
313-764-1361
BM

The University of Michigan–Flint
School of Management
Flint, Michigan 48502-2186
313-762-3164
BM

Michigan State University
College of Business
The Graduate School of Business
Administration
East Lansing, Michigan 48824
517-355-8377
BM

Middle Tennessee State University
School of Business
Murfreesboro, Tennessee 37132
615-898-2764
BM

University of Minnesota
School of Management
271 19th Avenue S.
Minneapolis, Minnesota 55455
612-625-0027
BM

University of Mississippi
School of Business Administration
University, Mississippi 38677
601-232-5820
BM

Mississippi State University
College of Business and Industry
Mississippi State, Mississippi
39762
601-325-2580
BM

University of Missouri–Columbia
College of Business and Public
Administration
107 Middlebush Hall
Columbia, Missouri 65211
314-882-6688
BM

University of Missouri–Kansas City
School of Business and Public
Administration
5100 Rockhill Road
Kansas City, Missouri 64110
816-276-1107
BM

University of Missouri–St. Louis
School of Business Administration
8001 Natural Bridge Road
St. Louis, Missouri 63121-4499
314-553-5886
BM

University of Montana
School of Business Administration
Missoula, Montana 59812
406-243-4831
BM

Montana State University
College of Business
Bozmen, Montana 59717-0001
406-994-4423
B

University of Montevallo
  Station 6450
  College of Business
  Montevallo, Alabama 35115
  205-665-6540
  B

Murray State University
  College of Business and Public
    Affairs
  Murray, Kentucky 42071
  502-762-4181
  BM

University of Nebraska–Lincoln
  College of Business Administration
  Lincoln, Nebraska 68588-0405
  402-472-1442
  BM

University of Nebraska at Omaha
  College of Business Administration
  Omaha, Nebraska 68182
  402-554-2303
  BM

University of Nevada, Reno
  College of Business Administration
  Reno, Nevada 89557
  702-784-4912
  BM

University of New Mexico
  The Robert O. Anderson School of
    Management
  The Robert O. Anderson Graduate
    School of Management
  Albuquerque, New Mexico 87131
  505-277-6471
  BM

New Mexico State University
  College of Business
    Administration and Economics
  Box 3AD
  Las Cruces, New Mexico 88003
  505-646-2821
  BM

University of New Orleans
  College of Business Administration
  New Orleans, Louisiana 70148
  504-286-6241
  BM

New York University
  College of Business and Public
    Administration
  800 Tisch Hall
  Washington Square
  New York, New York 10003
  212-998-4010
  B

New York University
  Graduate School of Business
    Administration
  100 Trinity Place
  New York, New York 10006
  212-285-6200
  M

Nicholls State University
  College of Business Administration
  P.O. Box 2015, NSU
  Thibodaux, Louisiana 70310
  504-448-4170
  BM

The University of North Carolina at
  Chapel Hill
  School of Business Administration
  CB 3490, Carroll Hall 012A
  Chapel Hill, North Carolina
    27599-3490
  919-962-3232
  BM

University of North Carolina at
  Charlotte
  College of Business Administration
  Charlotte, North Carolina 28223
  704-547-2165
  BM

University of North Carolina at
Greensboro
Joseph M. Bryan School of
Business and Economics
Greensboro, North Carolina 27412
919-334-5344
BM

North Carolina A & T State University
School of Business and Economics
Greensboro, North Carolina 27411
919-334-7632
B

University of North Dakota
College of Business and Public
Administration
Grand Forks, North Dakota 58202
701-777-2135
B

University of North Florida
College of Business Administration
4567 St. Johns Bluff Road, S.
Jacksonville, Florida 32216
904-646-2590
BM

University of North Texas
College of Business Administration
Denton, Texas 76203
817-565-3038
BM

Northeast Louisiana University
College of Business Administration
Monroe, Louisiana 71209
318-342-4190
BM

Northeastern University
College of Business Administration
202-Hayden Hall
360 Huntington Avenue
Boston, Massachusetts 02115
617-437-3239
BM

Northern Arizona University
College of Business Administration
C.U. Box 15066
Flagstaff, Arizona 86011
602-523-7345
BM

Northern Illinois University
College of Business
DeKalb, Illinois 60115
815-753-1755
BM

Northwestern University
J.L. Kellogg Graduate School of
Management
Leverone Hall
2001 Sheridan Road
Evanston, Illinois 60208
708-491-3300
M

University of Notre Dame
College of Business Administration
Notre Dame, Indiana 46556
219-239-7236
BM

Oakland University
School of Business Administration
Rochester, Michigan 48309-4401
313-370-3286
BM

The Ohio State University
College of Business Administration
1775 College Road
Columbus, Ohio 43210-1399
614-292-2666
BM

Ohio University
College of Business Administration
Athens, Ohio 45701
614-593-2002
BM

University of Oklahoma
College of Business Administration
307 W. Brooks, Room 208
Norman, Oklahoma 73019
405-325-3611
BM

Oklahoma State University
College of Business Administration
Stillwater, Oklahoma 74078-0555
405-624-5064
BM

Old Dominion University
College of Business and Public
Administration
Norfolk, Virginia 23529-0218
804-440-3521
BM

University of Oregon
Graduate School of Management
College of Business Administration
Eugene, Oregon 97403
503-686-3300
BM

Oregon State University
College of Business
Corvallis, Oregon 97331
503-754-2551
BM

University of the Pacific
School of Business and Public
Administration
Stockton, California 95211
209-946-2463
B

Pacific Lutheran University
School of Business Administration
Tacoma, Washington 98447
206-535-7251
BM

Pan American University
School of Business Administration
Edinburg, Texas 78539
512-381-3311
BM

University of Pennsylvania
The Wharton School
3620 Locust Walk
Philadelphia, Pennsylvania 19104
215-898-4851
BM

The Pennsylvania State University
College of Business Administration
801 Business Administration Bldg.
University Park, Pennsylvania
16802
814-863-0448
BM

University of Pittsburgh
Graduate School of Business
372 Mervis Hall
Pittsburgh, Pennsylvania 15260
412-648-1561
BM

University of Portland
School of Business Administration
Portland, Oregon 97203
503-283-7224
BM

Portland State University
School of Business Administration
P.O. Box 751
Portland, Oregon 97207
503-229-3716
BM

Purdue University
School of Management and
Krannert Graduate School of
Management
West Lafayette, Indiana 47907
317-494-4366
BM

Rensselaer Polytechnic Institute
School of Management
Troy, New York 12180
518-276-6802
BM

University of Rhode Island
College of Business Administration
301 Ballentine Hall
Kingston, Rhode Island 02881
401-792-2337
BM

University of Richmond
E. Clairborne Robins School of
Business
University of Richmond, Virginia
23173
804-289-8550
BM

University of Rochester
William E. Simon Graduate
School of Business
Administration
Rochester, New York 14627
716-275-3316
M

Rochester Institute of Technology
College of Business
One Lomb Memorial Drive
P.O.Box 9887
Rochester, New York 14623
716-475-6915
BM

Rollins College
Roy E. Crummer Graduate School
of Business
Winter Park, Florida 32789
407-646-2249
M

Rutgers–The State University of New
Jersey
Graduate School of Management
Newark, New Jersey 07102
201-648-5128
BM

Saint Cloud State University
College of Business
Saint Cloud, Minnesota 56301
612-255-3212
BM

St. John's University
Colleges of Business
Administration
Utopia and Grand Central Parkways
Jamaica, New York 11439
718-990-6477
BM

St. Louis University
School of Business Administration
3674 Lindell Boulevard
St. Louis, Missouri 63108
314-658-3833
BM

University of San Diego
School of Business Administration
San Diego, California 92110
619-260-4886
BM

San Diego State University
College of Business Administration
San Diego, California 92182
619-594-5301
BM

University of San Francisco
McLaren College of Business
San Francisco, California
94117-1040
415-666-6771
BM

San Francisco State University
School of Business
1600 Holloway Avenue
San Francisco, California 94132
415-338-2670
BM

San Jose State University
School of Business
1 Washington Square
San Jose, California 95192-0065
408-924-3400
BM

Santa Clara University
Leavey School of Business and
Administration
Santa Clara, California 95053
408-554-5423
BM

Seattle University
Albers School of Business
Seattle, Washington 98122
206-296-5701
BM

Seton Hall University
W. Paul Stillman School of
Business
South Orange, New Jersey 07079
201-761-9013
BM

Shippensburg University
College of Business
350 Shippen Hall
Shippensburg, Pennsylvania 17257
717-532-1435
B

University of South Alabama
College of Business and
Management Studies
Mobile, Alabama 36688
205-460-6419
BM

University of South Carolina
College of Business Administration
Graduate School of Business
Columbia, South Carolina 29208
803-777-3177
BM

University of South Dakota
School of Business
414 East Clark Street
Vermillion, South Dakota 57069
605-677-5455
BM

University of South Florida
College of Business Administration
4202 Fowler Avenue
Tampa, Florida 33620-5500
813-974-4281
BM

Southeastern Louisiana University
College of Business
P.O. Box 735, University Station
Hammond, Louisiana 70402
504-549-2258
BM

University of Southern California
Graduate School of Business
Administration
Hoffman Hall 800
Los Angeles, California
90089-1421
213-743-2431
BM

Southern Illinois University at
Carbondale
College of Business and
Administration
Carbondale, Illinois 62901
618-453-3328
BM

Southern Illinois University at
  Edwardsville
  School of Business
  Edwardsville, Illinois 62026
  618-692-3823
  BM

Southern Methodist University
  Edwin L. Cox School of Business
  Dallas, Texas 74275
  214-692-3012
  BM

University of Southern Mississippi
  College of Business Administration
  Southern Station Box 5021
  Hattiesburg, Mississippi 39406
  601-266-4659
  BM

Stanford University
  Graduate School of Business
  Stanford, California 94305-2391
  415-723-3951
  M

State University of New York at
  Albany
  School of Business
  1400 Washington Avenue
  Albany, New York 12222
  518-442-4910
  BM

State University of New York at
  Buffalo
  School of Management
  160 Jacobs Management Center
  Buffalo, New York 14260
  716-636-3222
  BM

Stephen F. Austin State University
  School of Business
  Nacogdoches, Texas 75962
  409-568-3101
  BM

Suffolk University
  School of Management
  Beacon Hill
  8 Ashburton Place
  Boston, Massachusetts 02108
  617-573-8300
  BM

Syracuse University
  School of Management
  Syracuse, New York 13244-2130
  315-443-3751
  BM

Temple University
  School of Business and
    Management
  Philadelphia, Pennsylvania 19122
  215-787-7676
  BM

University of Tennessee at
  Chattanooga
  School of Business Administration
  Chattanooga, Tennessee 37403
  615-755-4313
  BM

University of Tennessee, Knoxville
  College of Business Administration
  Knoxville, Tennessee 37996-0570
  615-974-5061
  BM

Tennessee Technological University
  College of Business Administration
  Cookeville, Tennessee 38505
  615-372-3372
  BM

The University of Texas at Arlington
  College of Business Administration
  P.O. Box 19377
  Arlington, Texas 76019
  817-273-2881
  BM

University of Texas at Austin
College of Business Administration
Graduate School of Business
Austin, Texas 78712
512-471-5921
BM

University of Texas at El Paso
College of Business Administration
El Paso, Texas 79968
915-747-5241
BM

The University of Texas at San
Antonio
College of Business
San Antonio, Texas 78285-0631
512-691-4313
BM

Texas A&M University
College of Business Administration
College Station, Texas 77843
409-845-4712
BM

Texas Christian University
M.J. Neeley School of Business
Fort Worth, Texas 76129
817-921-7526
BM

Texas Tech University
College of Business Administration
Lubbock, Texas 79409
806-742-3188
BM

University of Toledo
College of Business Administration
Toledo, Ohio 43606
419-537-2558
BM

Tulane University
A.B. Freeman School of Business
New Orleans, Louisiana
70118-5669
504-865-5407
BM

University of Tulsa
College of Business Administration
600 South College
Tulsa, Oklahoma 74104
918-592-6000
BM

University of Utah
Graduate School of Business and
College of Business
Salt Lake City, Utah 84112
801-581-7200
BM

Utah State University
College of Business
Logan, Utah 84322-3500
801-750-2272
BM

Vanderbilt University
Owen Graduate School of
Management
Nashville, Tennessee 37203
615-322-2316
M

University of Vermont
School of Business Administration
Mansfield House
Burlington, Vermont 05405
802-656-3177
BM

Villanova University
College of Commerce and Finance
Villanova, Pennsylvania 19085
215-645-4330
BM

University of Virginia
The Darden School
P.O. Box 6550
Charlottesville, Virginia 22906
804-924-7481
M

University of Virginia
McIntire School of Commerce
#236 Monroe Hall
Charlottesville, Virginia 22903
804-924-3176
BM

Virginia Commonwealth University
School of Business
Richmond, Virginia 23284-4000
804-367-1595
BM

Virginia Polytechnic Institute and
State University
College of Business
Blacksburg, Virginia 24061
703-231-6601
BM

Wake Forest University
Babcock Graduate's School of
Management
7659 Reynolds Station
Winston-Salem, North Carolina
27109
919-761-5418
M

Wake Forest University
School of Business and
Accountancy
P.O. Box 7285, Reynolds Station
Winston-Salem, North Carolina
27109
919-761-5304
B

University of Washington
School and Graduate School of
Business Administration, DJ-10
Seattle, Washington 98195
206-543-4752
BM

Washington University
School of Business and Public
Administration
The Graduate School of Business
Administration
St. Louis, Missouri 63130
314-889-6344
BM

Washington and Lee University
School of Commerce, Economics,
and Politics
Lexington, Virginia 24450
703-463-8602
B

Washington State University
College of Business and Economics
Pullman, Washington 99164-4720
509-335-3596
BM

Wayne State University
School of Business Administration
Detroit, Michigan 48202
313-577-4501
BM

West Georgia College
School of Business
Carrollton, Georgia 30118
404-836-6467
B

West Virginia University
College of Business and Economics
Morgantown, West Virginia
26506-6025
304-293-4092
BM

Western Carolina University
School of Business
Cullowhee, North Carolina 28723
704-227-7401
BM

Western Illinois University
College of Business
Macomb, Illinois 61455
309-298-2442
BM

Western Kentucky University
College of Business Administration
Bowling Green, Kentucky 42101
502-745-6311
B

Western Michigan University
College of Business
Kalamazoo, Michigan 49008
616-387-7047
BM

Wichita State University
W. Frank Barton School of
Business
Wichita, Kansas 67208
316-689-3200
BM

Winthrop College
School of Business Administration
Rock Hill, South Carolina 29730
803-323-2185
BM

University of Wisconsin–La Crosse
College of Business Administration
1725 State Street
La Crosse, Wisconsin 54601
608-785-8090
BM

University of Wisconsin–Madison
School of Business
Madison, Wisconsin 53706
608-262-1553
BM

University of Wisconsin–Milwaukee
School of Business Administration
P.O. Box 742
Milwaukee, Wisconsin 53201
414-963-4235
BM

University of Wisconsin–Oshkosh
College of Business Administration
Oshkosh, Wisconsin 54901
414-424-1424
BM

University of Wisconsin–Whitewater
College of Business and Economics
Whitewater, Wisconsin 53190
414-472-1343
BM

Wright State University
College of Business and
Administration
Dayton, Ohio 45435
513-873-3242
BM

University of Wyoming
College of Commerce and Industry
Laramie, Wyoming 82071
307-766-4194
BM

AMERICAN ASSEMBLY OF COLLEGIATE SCHOOLS OF BUSINESS ACCREDITED ACCOUNTING PROGRAMS

The following schools are accredited for the type of accounting program(s) indicated in the last line of each listing. A = baccalaureate degrees with emphasis in accounting; B = MBA degrees with emphasis in accounting; and C = master of accounting degrees.

University of Akron
Accounting Department
College of Business Administration
Akron, Ohio 44325
216-375-7589
AB

University of Alabama
School of Accountancy
P.O. Drawer AC
Tuscaloosa, Alabama 35487-1399
205-348-6131
AC

University of Alabama at Birmingham
Department of Accounting
School of Business
University Station
Birmingham, Alabama 35294
205-934-8820
AC

University of Alaska–Fairbanks
Department of Accounting
School of Management
Fairbanks, Alaska 99775
907-474-7461
A

Arizona State University
Department of Accounting
College of Business
Tempe, Arizona 85287
602-965-3631
AC

University of Arkansas
Department of Accounting
College of Business Administration
Fayetteville, Arkansas 72701
501-575-4051
AC

Baruch College–The City University of New York
Department of Accountancy
School of Business and Public Administration
17 Lexington Avenue
New York, New York 10010
212-725-3327
AB

Baylor University
Accounting Department
Hankamer School of Business
Box 6278
Waco, Texas 76798
817-755-3536
A

Bradley University
Department of Accounting
College of Business Administration
Peoria, Illinois 61625
309-677-2289
A

Case Western University
Department of Accountancy
Weatherhead School of Management
Cleveland, Ohio 44106
216-368-2074
AC

Central Michigan University
Department of Accounting
School of Business Administration
Mt. Pleasant, Michigan 48859
517-774-3796
A

University of Chicago
Institute of Professional Accounting
Graduate School of Business
1101 East 58th Street
Chicago, Illinois 60637
312-702-7261
B

Clemson University
School of Accountancy
College of Commerce and Industry
Clemson, South Carolina
29634-1303
803-656-3265
AC

Cleveland State University
James J. Nance College of
Business Administration
1983 E. 24th Street UC 579
Cleveland, Ohio 44115
216-687-4721
AC

College of William and Mary
School of Business Administration
Williamsburg, Virginia 23185
804-253-4433
A

University of Connecticut
Department of Accounting
School of Business Administration
Storrs, Connecticut 06268
203-486-3018
AB

Creighton University
Department of Accounting
College of Business Administration
Omaha, Nebraska 68178
402-280-2602
A

University of Delaware
Department of Accounting
College of Business and Economics
Newark, Delaware 19716
302-451-2961
AC

DePaul University
School of Accountancy
College of Commerce
25 East Jackson Boulevard
Chicago, Illinois 60604
312-341-8770
ABC

University of Florida
Fisher School of Accounting
Gainesville, Florida 32611
904-392-0155
ABC

Florida International University
School of Accounting
College of Business Administration
Tamiami Trail
Miami, Florida 33199
305-554-2581
AC

Florida State University
Department of Accounting
College of Business
Tallahassee, Florida 32306-1042
904-644-2771
AC

Georgia State University
  School of Accountancy
  College of Business Administration
  University Plaza
  Atlanta, Georgia 30303-3083
  404-651-2616
  ABC

University of Houston–Clear Lake
  School of Business and Public
    Administration
  2700 Bay Area Boulevard
  Houston, Texas 77058
  713-488-9374
  AC

University of Houston–University Park
  Department of Accountancy and
    Taxation
  College of Business Administration
  370 Melcher Hall
  4800 Calhoun
  Houston, Texas 77004
  713-749-7216
  ABC

Howard University
  Department of Accounting
  School of Business and Public
    Administration
  Washington, D.C. 20059
  202-636-5165
  A

University of
  Illinois–Urbana-Champaign
  Department of Accountancy
  College of Commerce and
    Business Administration
  360 Commerce West
  1260 S. Sixth Street
  Champaign, Illinois 61820
  217-333-2451
  AC

James Madison University
  School of Accounting
  College of Business
  Harrisonburg, Virginia 22807
  703-568-6607
  AC

Kansas State University
  Department of Accounting
  College of Business Administration
  Manhattan, Kansas 66506
  913-532-6184
  AC

University of Kentucky
  Department of Accounting
  College of Business and Economics
  Lexington, Kentucky 40506-0034
  606-257-1876
  AC

Lehigh University
  Department of Accounting
  College of Business and Economics
  Bethlehem, Pennsylvania 18015
  215-758-3450
  A

Louisiana Tech University
  School of Professional
    Accountancy
  Ruston, Louisiana 71272
  318-257-2822
  ABC

University of Louisville
  Department of Accounting
  School of Business
  Louisville, Kentucky 40292
  502-588-5847
  A

Memphis State University
School of Accountancy
Fogelman College of Business and
Economics
Memphis, Tennessee 38152
901-454-2445
ABC

University of Miami
Department of Accounting
School of Business Administration
P.O. Box 248031
Coral Gables, Florida 33124
305-284-5428
AC

Miami University
Department of Accountancy
School of Business Administration
Oxford, Ohio 45056
513-529-6200
AC

Michigan State University
Department of Accounting
College of Business
East Lansing, Michigan 48824
517-355-3388
AB

The University of Mississippi
School of Accountancy
109 Conner Hall
University, Mississippi 38677
601-232-7468
AC

University of Missouri–Columbia
School of Accountancy
312 Middlebush Hall
Columbia, Missouri 65211
314-882-3478
AC

University of Nebraska–Lincoln
School of Accountancy
College of Business Administration
Lincoln, Nebraska 68588-0488
402-472-2337
AC

University of New Orleans
Department of Accounting
College of Business Administration
New Orleans, Louisiana 70148
504-286-6244
A

New York University
Accounting Department
Graduate School of Business
100 Trinity Place
New York, New York 10006
212-285-6260
ABC

University of North Carolina
Accounting Department
College of Business Administration
Charlotte, North Carolina 28223
704-547-2446
A

North Carolina A&T State University
Accounting Department
School of Business and Economics
Greensboro, North Carolina 27411
919-334-7525
A

North Texas State University
Department of Accounting
College of Business Administration
Denton, Texas 76203-3677
817-565-3095
AC

Northern Illinois University
Department of Accountancy
College of Business
DeKalb, Illinois 60115
815-753-1250
AC

University of Notre Dame
Department of Accountancy
College of Business Administration
Notre Dame, Indiana 46556
219-239-7324
A

The Ohio State University
Faculty of Accounting and
Management Information
Systems
College of Business
1775 College Road
Columbus, Ohio 43210
614-292-2081
AB

University of Oklahoma
School of Accounting
307 W. Brooks, Room 200
Norman, Oklahoma 73019
405-325-4221
AC

Oklahoma State University
School of Accounting
College of Business Administration
Stillwater, Oklahoma 74078-0555
405-624-5123
AC

Old Dominion University
Department of Accounting
School of Business
Norfolk, Virginia 23508
804-440-3529
A

University of Oregon
Department of Accounting
College of Business Administration
Eugene, Oregon 97403-1208
503-606-3320
A

Oregon State University
Department of Accounting
College of Business
Corvallis, Oregon 97331-2603
503-754-4276
A

Pacific Lutheran University
Accounting Program
School of Business Administration
Tacoma, Washington 98447
206-535-7308
A

The Pennsylvania State University
Department of Accounting and
Management Information
Systems
College of Business Administration
206 Business Administration Bldg.
III
University Park, Pennsylvania
16802
814-865-1809
ABC

Portland State University
Department of Accounting
School of Business Administration
Portland, Oregon 97203
503-464-3713
A

University of Richmond
Accounting Department
The E. Clairborne Robins School
of Business
Richmond, Virginia 23173
804-285-8593
A

San Diego State University
School of Accountancy
San Diego, California 92182-0082
619-265-4307
AC

University of South Carolina
College of Business Administration
Graduate School of Business
Columbia, South Carolina 29208
803-777-7440
AC

University of South Florida
School of Accountancy
College of Business Administration
Tampa, Florida 33620-5500
813-974-4186
AC

Southern Illinois University at
Carbondale
Department of Accountancy
College of Business and
Administration
Carbondale, Illinois 62901
618-453-2289
AC

Southern Illinois University at
Edwardsville
Accounting Department
School of Business
Edwardsville, Illinois 62026-1104
618-692-2633
A

State University of New York at
Buffalo
Department of Accounting
School of Management
Buffalo, New York 14260
716-636-3276
AB

University of Tennessee at Knoxville
Department of Accounting and
Business Law

College of Business Administration
Knoxville, Tennessee 37996-0560
615-974-2386
ABC

Tennessee Technological University
Accounting and Finance
Department
College of Business Administration
Cookeville, Tennessee 38505
615-528-3133
A

Texas A&M University
Department of Accounting
College Station, Texas 77843-4353
409-845-5014
AC

The University of Texas at Arlington
Department of Accountancy
College of Business
P.O. Box 19468
Arlington, Texas 76019
817-273-2044
ABC

University of Texas at El Paso
Department of Accounting
College of Business Administration
El Paso, Texas 79968-0542
915-747-5192
AC

Texas Tech University
Area of Accounting
College of Business Administration
Lubbock, Texas 79409-4320
806-742-3181
AC

University of Utah
  School of Accounting
  College of Business and Graduate
    School of Business
  KDGB 108
  Salt Lake City, Utah 84322-3540
  801-581-7723
  AC

Utah State University
  School of Accountancy
  College of Business
  UMC 35
  Logan, Utah 84322-3540
  801-750-2331
  AC

Villanova University
  Department of Accountancy
  College of Commerce and Finance
  Villanova, Pennsylvania 19085
  215-645-4340

University of Virginia
  Area of Accounting
  McIntire School of Commerce
  Monroe Hall
  Charlottesville, Virginia
    22903-2493
  804-924-3281
  AC

Virginia Commonwealth University
  Department of Accounting
  School of Business
  1015 Floyd Avenue
  Richmond, Virginia 23284-0001
  804-257-1608
  AC

Virginia Polytechnic Institute and
  State University
  Department of Accounting
  College of Business
  222 Burrus Hall
  Blacksburg, Virginia 24061
  703-961-6591
  AC

Wake Forest University
  School of Business and
    Accountancy
  Winston-Salem, North Carolina
    27109
  919-761-5784
  A

University of Washington
  Department of Accounting
  Graduate School and School of
    Business Administration
  DJ-10
  Seattle, Washington 98195
  206-543-4368
  AC

Washington State University
  Department of Accounting and
    Business Law
  College of Business and Economics
  Pullman, Washington 99164-4720
  509-335-8541
  AC

STATE BOARDS OF ACCOUNTANCY

For detailed information about the accountancy laws in your state, including the requirements for becoming a CPA, call or write your state board of accountancy at the following addresses.

Alabama State Board of Public
Accountancy
12 Commerce Row
529 South Perry Street
Montgomery, AL 36104-3503
(205) 834-7651

Alaska State Board of Public
Accountancy
Department of Commerce
Div. of Occ. Licensing, Pouch D
Juneau, AK 99811-0800
(907) 465-2580

Arizona State Board of Accountancy
3110 North Nineteenth Avenue
Suite 140
Phoenix, AZ 85015-6038
(602) 255-3648

Arkansas State Board of Accountancy
1515 West Seventh Street, Suite 320
Little Rock, AR 72201-3934
(501) 682-1520

California State Board of Accountancy
2135 Butano Drive, Suite 112
Sacramento, CA 95825-0451
(916) 920-7121

Colorado State Board of Accountancy
1525 Sherman Street, Room 617
Denver, CO 80203-1719
(303) 866-2869

Connecticut State Board of
Accountancy
Secretary of the State
30 Trinity Street
Hartford, CT 06106
(203) 566-7835

Delaware State Board of Accountancy
Margaret O'Neill Building
P.O. Box 1401
Dover, DE 19903
(302) 736-4522

District of Columbia Board of
Accountancy
Dept. of Consumer & Regulatory Aff.
614 H Street, NW, Room 923
Washington,DC 20515-6019
(202) 727-7468

Florida Board of Accountancy
4001 N.W. 43d Street,Suite 16
Gainesville, FL 32606-4598
(904) 336-2165

Georgia State Board of Accountancy
166 Pryor Street, SW
Atlanta,GA 30303
(404) 656-3941

Guam Territorial Board of Public
Accountancy
c/o Pickens Borja & Filush, P.C.
590 South Marine Drive, Suite 619
Tamuning, GU 96910
(671) 646-6987

Hawaii Board of Public Accountancy
Department of Commerce and
Consumer Affairs
P.O. Box 3469
Honolulu, HI 96801-3469
(808) 548-7471

Idaho State Board of Accountancy
500 South Tenth Street, Suite 104
Statehouse Mail
Boise, ID 83720
(208) 334-2490

Illinois Committee on Accountancy
Univ. of Illinois
Urbana-Champaign
10 Admin. Bldg., 506 South
Wright Street
Urbana, IL 61801-3260
(217) 333-1565

Illinois Department of Professional
Regulation
Public Accountancy Section
320 West Washington Street, 3d
Floor
Springfield, IL 62786-0001
(217) 785-0800

Indiana State Board of Public
Accountancy
Professional Licensing Agency
1021 State Office Building
Indianapolis, IN 46204
(317) 232-3898

Iowa Accountancy Examining Board
1918 S.E. Hulsizer Avenue
Ankeny, IA 50021
(515) 281-4126

Kansas Board of Accountancy
Landon State Office Building
900 S.W. Jackson, Suite 556
Topeka, KS 66612-1220
(913) 296-2162

Kentucky State Board of Accountancy
332 West Broadway, Suite 310
Louisville, KY 40202-2115
(502) 588-3037

State Board of CPAs of Louisiana
1515 World Trade Center
2 Canal Street
New Orleans, LA 70130
(504) 566-1244

Maine State Board of Accountancy
Dept. of Prof. & Fin. Reg., Div. of
Lic. & Enf., State House Station 35
Augusta, ME 04333
(207) 582-8723

Maryland State Board of Public
Accountancy
501 St. Paul Place, 9th Floor
Baltimore, MD 21202-2222
(301) 333-6322

Massachusetts Board of Public
Accountancy
Saltonstall Building, Room 1514
100 Cambridge Street
Boston, MA 02202-0001
(617) 727-1753

Michigan Board of Accountancy
Dept. of Licensing & Regulation
P.O. Box 30018
Lansing, MI 48909-7518
(517) 373-0682

Minnesota State Board of
Accountancy
133 East 7th Street, 3d Floor
St. Paul, MN 55101
(612) 296-7937

Mississippi State Board of Public
Accountancy
961 Highway 80 East
Clinton, MS 39056-5246
(601) 924-8457

Missouri State Board of Accountancy
P.O. Box 613
Jefferson City, MO 65102-0613
(314) 751-0012

Montana State Board of Public
Accountants
1424 9th Avenue
Helena, MT 59620-0407
(406) 444-3739

Nebraska State Board of Public
Accountancy
P.O. Box 94725
Lincoln, NE 68509-4725
(402) 471-3595

Nevada State Board of Accountancy
1 East Liberty Street, Suite 311
Reno, NV 89501-2110
(702) 786-0231

New Hampshire Board of
Accountancy
57 Regional Drive
Concord, NH 03301
(603) 271-3286

New Jersey State Board of
Accountancy
1100 Raymond Blvd., Room 507-A
Newark, NJ 07102-5205
(201) 648-3240

New Mexico State Board of Public
Accountancy
4125 Carlisle NE
Albuquerque, NM 87107
(505) 841-6524

New York State Board for Public
Accountancy
State Education Department
Cultural Education Center, Rm.
9A47
Albany, NY 12230-0001
(518) 474-3836

North Carolina State Board of CPA
Examiners
1101 Oberlin Road, Suite 104
P.O. Box 12827
Raleigh, NC 27605-2827
(919) 733-4222

North Dakota State Board of
Accountancy
Box 8104, University Station
Grand Forks, ND 58202
(701) 777-3869

Accountancy Board of Ohio
77 South High Street, 18th Floor
Columbus, OH 43266-0301
(614) 466-4135

Oklahoma State Board of Public
Accountancy
4545 Lincoln Blvd., Suite 165
Oklahoma City, OK 73105-3413
(405) 521-2397

Oregon State Board of Accountancy
Commerce Building, First Floor
Salem, OR 97310-0001
(503) 378-4181

Pennsylvania State Board of
Accountancy
613 Transportation & Safety Bldg.
P.O. Box 2649
Harrisburg, PA 17105-2649
(717) 783-1404

Puerto Rico Board of Accountancy
Box 3271
San Juan, PR 00904-3271
(809) 722-2122

Rhode Island Board of Accountancy
Dept. of Business Regulation
233 Richmond Street, Suite 236
Providence, RI 02903-4236
(401) 277-3185

South Carolina Board of Accountancy
Dutch Plaza, Suite 260
800 Dutch Square Blvd.
Columbia, SC 29210
(803) 737-9266

South Dakota Board of Accountancy
301 East 14th Street, Suite 200
Sioux Falls, SD 57104
(605) 339-6746

Tennessee State Board of Accountancy
500 James Robertson Parkway
2d Floor
Nashville, TN 37219
(615) 741-2550

Texas State Board of Public
Accountancy
1033 La Posada, Suite 340
Austin, TX 78752-3892
(512) 451-0241

Utah Board of Accountancy
160 East 300 South
P.O. Box 45802
Salt Lake City, UT 84145-0802
(801) 530-6628

Vermont Board of Public Accountancy
Pavilion Office Bldg.
Montpelier, VT 05602
(802) 828-2363

Virginia Board for Accountancy
3600 West Broad Street
Richmond, VA 23230-4915
(804) 367-8505

Virgin Islands Board of Public
Accountancy
1B King Street
Christiansted
St. Croix, VI 00820-4933
(809) 773-0096

Washington State Board of
Accountancy
210 East Union, Suite H
P.O. Box 9131
Olympia, WA 98504-2321
(206) 753-2585

West Virginia Board of Accountancy
201 L & S Building
812 Quarrier Street
Charleston, WV 25301-2617
(304) 348-3557

Wisconsin Accounting Examining
Board
1400 East Washington Avenue
P.O. Box 8935
Madison, WI 53708-8935
(608) 266-3020

Wyoming Board of Certified Public
Accountants
Barrett Building, 3d Floor
Cheyenne, WY 82002-0001
(307) 777-7551

STATE PROFESSIONAL ORGANIZATIONS OF CPAs

As local professional societies, state CPA organizations maintain codes of professional ethics, conduct professional development courses, and publish newsletters and journals. They usually can supply information on scholarships and employment opportunities in the state and can answer questions about the professions.

Alabama Society of CPAs
P.O. Box 4187
Montgomery, AL 36103
(205) 834-7650

Alaska Society of CPAs
3900 Arctic, #202
Anchorage, AK 99503
(907) 562-4334

Arizona Society of CPAs
426 North 44th Street
Suite 250
Phoenix, AZ 85008-6501
(602) 273-0100

Arkansas Society of CPAs
415 North McKinley Street
Little Rock, AR 72205-3022
(501) 664-8739

California Society of CPAs
275 Shoreline Drive
Redwood City, CA 94065
(415) 594-1717

Colorado Society of CPAs
7720 East Belleview Avenue
Englewood,CO 80111
(303) 773-2877

Connecticut Society of CPAs
179 Allyn Street
Suite 201
Hartford, CT 06103-1491
(203) 525-1153

Delaware Society of CPAs
28 The Commons
3520 Silverside Road
Wilmington, DE 19810
(302) 478-7442

District of Columbia Institute of CPAs
1666 K Street, NW
Suite 907
Washington, DC 20006
(202) 659-9183

Florida Institute of CPAs
P.O. Box 5437
Tallahassee, FL 32314-5437
(904) 224-2727

Georgia Society of CPAs
3340 Peachtree Road, NE
Suite 2750, Tower Place
Atlanta, GA 30326
(404) 231-8676

Guam Society of CPAs
P.O. Box P
Agana, GU 96910

Hawaii Society of CPAs
P.O. Box 1754
Honolulu, HI 96806
(808) 537-9475

Idaho Society of CPAs
323 West Idaho
Suite 1
Boise, ID 83702
(208) 344-6261

Illinois CPA Society
222 South Riverside Plaza
Chicago, IL 60606
(312) 993-0393

Indiana CPA Society
P.O. Box 68847
Indianapolis, IN 46268
(317) 872-5184

Iowa Society of CPAs
950 Office Park Road
Suite 300
West Des Moines, IA 50265
(515) 223-8161

Kansas Society of CPAs
P.O. Box 5654
Topeka, KS 66605-0654
(913) 267-6460

Kentucky Society of CPAs
310 West Liberty Street
Room 604
Louisville, KY 40202
(502) 589-9239

Society of Louisiana CPAs
2400 Veterans Boulevard
Suite 500
Kenner, LA 70062
(504) 469-7930

Maine Society of CPAs
Box 7406 DTS
Portland, ME 04112
(207) 772-9639

Maryland Association of CPAs
P.O. Box 484
Lutherville, MD 21093
(301) 296-6250

Massachusetts Society of CPAs
105 Chauncy Street
10th Floor
Boston, MA 02111
(617) 556-4000

Michigan Association of CPAs
P.O. Box 9054
Farmington Hills, MI 48333
(313) 855-2288

Minnesota Society of CPAs
N.W. Financial Center
Suite 1230
7900 Xerexes Avenue South
Minneapolis, MN 55431
(612) 831-2707

Mississippi Society of CPAs
P.O. Box 16630
Jackson, MS 39236
(601) 366-3473

Missouri Society of CPAs
P.O. Box 27342
St. Louis, MO 63141
(314) 997-7966

Montana Society of CPAs
P.O. Box 138
Helena, MT 59624-0138
(406) 442-7301

Nebraska Society of CPAs
635 South 14th Street
Suite 330
Lincoln, NE 68508
(402) 476-8482

Nevada Society of CPAs
5270 Neil Road
Suite 102
Reno, NV 89502
(702) 826-6800

New Hampshire Society of CPAs
3 Executive Park Drive
Bedford, NH 03102
(603) 622-1999

New Jersey Society of CPAs
425 Eagle Rock Avenue
Roseland, NJ 07068
(201) 226-4494

New Mexico Society of CPAs
300 San Mateo, NE
Suite 101
Albuquerque, NM 87108
(505) 262-1926

New York State Society of CPAs
200 Park Avnue
10th Floor
New York, NY 10166-0010
(212) 973-8300

North Carolina Association of CPAs
P.O. Box 80188
Raleigh, NC 27623
(919) 469-1040

North Dakota Society of CPAs
Box 8104, University Station
Grand Forks, ND 58202
(701) 777-3869

Ohio Society of CPAs
P.O. Box 1810
Dublin, OH 43017
(614) 764-2727

Oklahoma Society of CPAs
128 West Hefner Road
Oklahoma City, OK 73114
(405) 478-4484

Oregon Society of CPAs
10206 Southwest Laurel Street
Beaverton, OR 97005-3209
(503) 641-7200

Pennsylvania Institute of CPAs
1608 Walnut Street
3d Floor
Philadelphia, PA 19103
(215) 735-2635

Colegio de Contadores Publicos
Autorizados de Puerto Rico
Apartado Postal 71352
San Juan, Puerto Rico 00936-1352
(809) 754-1950

Rhode Island Society of CPAs
One Franklin Square
Providence, RI 02903
(401) 331-5720

South Carolina Association of CPAs
570 Chris Drive
West Columbia, SC 29169
(803) 791-4181

South Dakota Society of CPAs
P.O. Box 1798
Sioux Falls, SD 57101-1798
(605) 334-3848

Tennessee Society of CPAs
P.O. Box 596
Brentwood, TN 37024-0596
(615) 377-3825

Texas Society of CPAs
1421 West Mockingbird Lane
Suite 100
Dallas, TX 75247
(214) 689-6000

Utah Association of CPAs
455 East 400 South
Suite 202
Salt Lake City, UT 84111
(801) 359-3533

Vermont Society of CPAs
P.O. Box 780
Montipelier, VT 05601
(802) 229-4939

Virginia Society of CPAs
P.O. Box 31635
Richmond, VA 23294
(804) 270-5344

Virgin Islands Society of CPAs
P.O. Box Y
Christiansted
St. Croix, VI 00822
(809) 773-4305

Washington Society of CPAs
902 140th Avenue, NE
Bellevue, WA 98005
(206) 644-4800

West Virginia Society of CPAs
P.O. Box 1142
Charleston, WV 25324
(304) 342-5461

Wisconsin Institute of CPAs
P.O. Box 1010
Brookfield, WI 53008
(414) 785-0445

Wyoming Society of CPAs
P.O. Box 966
Cheyenne, WY 82003
(307) 634-7039

VGM CAREER BOOKS

OPPORTUNITIES IN
Available in both paperback and hardbound editions
Accounting Careers
Acting Careers
Advertising Careers
Aerospace Careers
Agriculture Careers
Airline Careers
Animal and Pet Care
Appraising Valuation Science
Architecture
Automotive Service
Banking
Beauty Culture
Biological Sciences
Biotechnology Careers
Book Publishing Careers
Broadcasting Careers
Building Construction Trades
Business Communication Careers
Business Management
Cable Television
Carpentry Careers
Chemical Engineering
Chemistry Careers
Child Care Careers
Chiropractic Health Care
Civil Engineering Careers
Commercial Art and Graphic Design
Computer Aided Design and Computer
  Aided Mfg.
Computer Maintenance Careers
Computer Science Careers
Counseling & Development
Crafts Careers
Culinary Careers
Dance
Data Processing Careers
Dental Care
Drafting Careers
Electrical Trades
Electronic and Electrical Engineering
Energy Careers
Engineering Careers
Engineering Technology Careers
Environmental Careers
Eye Care Careers
Fashion Careers
Fast Food Careers
Federal Government Careers
Film Careers
Financial Careers
Fire Protection Services
Fitness Careers
Food Services
Foreign Language Careers
Forestry Careers
Gerontology Careers
Government Service
Graphic Communications
Health and Medical Careers
High Tech Careers
Home Economics Careers
Hospital Administration
Hotel & Motel Management
Human Resources Management Careers

Industrial Design
Information Systems Careers
Insurance Careers
Interior Design
International Business
Journalism Careers
Landscape Architecture
Laser Technology
Law Careers
Law Enforcement and Criminal Justice
Library and Information Science
Machine Trades
Magazine Publishing Careers
Management
Marine & Maritime Careers
Marketing Careers
Materials Science
Mechanical Engineering
Medical Technology Careers
Microelectronics
Military Careers
Modeling Careers
Music Careers
Newspaper Publishing Careers
Nursing Careers
Nutrition Careers
Occupational Therapy Careers
Office Occupations
Opticianry
Optometry
Packaging Science
Paralegal Careers
Paramedical Careers
Part-time & Summer Jobs
Performing Arts Careers
Petroleum Careers
Pharmacy Careers
Photography
Physical Therapy Careers
Physician Careers
Plumbing & Pipe Fitting
Podiatric Medicine
Printing Careers
Property Management Careers
Psychiatry
Psychology
Public Health Careers
Public Relations Careers
Purchasing Careers
Real Estate
Recreation and Leisure
Refrigeration and Air Conditioning
  Trades
Religious Service
Restaurant Careers
Retailing
Robotics Careers
Sales Careers
Sales & Marketing
Secretarial Careers
Securities Industry
Social Science Careers
Social Work Careers
Speech-Language Pathology Careers
Sports & Athletics
Sports Medicine
State and Local Government

Teaching Careers
Technical Communications
Telecommunications
Television and Video Careers
Theatrical Design & Production
Transportation Careers
Travel Careers
Veterinary Medicine Careers
Vocational and Technical Careers
Welding Careers
Word Processing
Writing Careers
Your Own Service Business

CAREERS IN
Accounting
Advertising
Business
Communications
Computers
Education
Engineering
Health Care
Science

CAREER DIRECTORIES
Careers Encyclopedia
Occupational Outlook Handbook

CAREER PLANNING
Admissions Guide to Selective
  Business Schools
Career Planning and Development for
  College Students and Recent Graduates
Careers Checklists
Careers for Bookworms and
  Other Literary Types
Careers for Sports Nuts
Handbook of Business and
  Management Careers
Handbook of Scientific and
  Technical Careers
How to Change Your Career
How to Get and Get Ahead
  On Your First Job
How to Get People to Do Things Your
  Way
How to Have a Winning Job Interview
How to Land a Better Job
How to Make the Right Career Moves
How to Prepare for College
How to Run Your Own Home Business
How to Write a Winning Résumé
Joyce Lain Kennedy's Career Book
Life Plan
Planning Your Career of Tomorrow
Planning Your College Education
Planning Your Military Career
Planning Your Young Child's Education

SURVIVAL GUIDES
Dropping Out or Hanging In
High School Survival Guide
College Survival Guide

VGM Career Horizons
A Division of National Textbook Company
4255 West Touhy Avenue
Lincolnwood, Illinois 60646-1975 U.S.A.